GENESIS

Book 1

Paul Sutliff

Copyright © 2024 Sutliffian Press

All rights reserved.

No part of this book may be reproduced, stored in a retrieval system, or transmitted by any means, electronic, mechanical, photocopying, recording, or otherwise, without written permission from the author.

ISBN (Paperback): 979-8-9919700-9-9
ISBN (eBook): 979-8-9919700-8-2

Forward

This book is dedicated to those who are disciples in Christ. It was written for YOU! You are about to embark on a journey of depth in scripture reading. Each day's devotional was part of my personal study. I spent the time to not only read the scripture, but to look at commentaries, to study words and their meanings. I looked at context. Asked questions. Why? Because I believe the Word of God is so important, we have to dig into it to get as much as we can out of it.

What appears a short reading actually takes me about an hour. Prayer, reading His Word, studying the passages, making sure I don't go to fast, have done one important thing to my life. I hold each reading in my heart most of the day. Better yet, each reading serves to arm me for battle, by making scripture not only real, but places the Word in my heart so that I may give answers to those who have questions.

For those struggling with anything some call addictions, which I call binding sin, I believe a daily deep-dive into HIS Word, is the solution. You want out of the sin that binds you to return to it? Grab one of these devotionals. Dig into the Word of God, pray and meditate on what you read. I promise your life will be better. I can say this because my life blossomed as if I had no clue to the wonders of God, before I started this part of my life.

For those scared of doing anything in depth – I am a Special Education Teacher. I write to average people, not scholars. This book was meant for you. It is purposefully written simply for the intent of sharing the deepness and joy of reading God's Word.

If you are a pastor or chaplain doing a prison ministry and are looking for a discount on books. Please contact me at Berean_research@yahoo.com.

DAY #1
GENESIS 1:1-2

1   In the beginning God created the heaven and the earth.
2   And the earth was without form, and void; and darkness *was* upon the face of the deep. And the Spirit of God moved upon the face of the waters.

God is the beginning of all that exists. He was here before the formation of the world. We should marvel that His Word here, written by Moses thousands of years ago beats the claim that the universe or something else is eternal and not God. These concepts came much later. Modern man wants to promote his own existence as superior to God. But that would not be possible if God existed before. Can a man claim that he is the beginning? No.

Can a man claim that he created the heavens? Note the plural use here. Heavens meaning: 1) the air around us, the layers of breathable air; 2) outer space where there are moons, stars, planets, and galaxies; 3) the place of reward for His gift of eternal life, the place where God's throne is, the place Jesus described as "my Father's House."

No man can claim he created the earth and all that is there in, and upon it. God was before. He created all that was created. Some may ask, how could God move on waters before, before there was earth? The best way to explain this is to reflect that this is an attempt to explain God and his movement as fluid. The word "water" in the Bible is compared to "grace." Even before the creation of the earth, before the creation of man, God moved in grace. His mercy, His depth of forgiveness is beyond our scope of understanding. His love reaches beyond anything we can imagine.

Dear Lord Jesus,

How is it that You love us so, when we are so rebellious and often choose not the things which You desire? Lord, You know our hearts. You know where we are in truth. No mask that we can put on hides our true nature from You. Lord, call each and every soul around me to a love of You. Call them to see Your mercy and understanding are far greater than anything they imagined. Lord, may I be one of those You use to draw others to You.

In Jesus name, Amen.

DAY #2
GENESIS 1:3-5

3   And God said, Let there be light: and there was light.
4   And God saw the light, that *it was* good: and God divided the light from the darkness.
5   And God called the light Day, and the darkness he called Night. And the evening and the morning were the first day.

God created light first not because he needed it, but because without light, the things he was about to create, could not survive. This is before the creation of the sun and the moon. Time has a whole other concept without the earth rotating. This was before that even happened. Jesus said in John 8:12, "I am the light of the world." The light of Jesus precedes the light created. Jesus being the "light of the world" created light so that all of creation yet to come can live and thrive. This is love.

Dear Lord Jesus,

You loved us even before we existed. You provided every little thing needed for us to live. But you went farther and prepared a world we could grow and become bigger. Even before the creation of earth, you loved us. How is it you loved us so? Lord, work on me. Make me a more loving person that those I encounter may find a way to you.

In Jesus name, Amen.

DAY #3
GENESIS 1:6-13

6   And God said, Let there be a firmament in the midst of the waters, and let it divide the waters from the waters.
7   And God made the firmament, and divided the waters which *were* under the firmament from the waters which *were* above the firmament: and it was so.
8   And God called the firmament Heaven. And the evening and the morning were the second day.

9   And God said, Let the waters under the heaven be gathered together unto one place, and let the dry *land* appear: and it was so.

10   And God called the dry *land* Earth; and the gathering together of the waters called he Seas: and God saw that *it was* good.

11   And God said, Let the earth bring forth grass, the herb yielding seed, *and* the fruit tree yielding fruit after his kind, whose seed *is* in itself, upon the earth: and it was so.

12   And the earth brought forth grass, *and* herb yielding seed after his kind, and the tree yielding fruit, whose seed *was* in itself, after his kind: and God saw that *it was* good.

13   And the evening and the morning were the third day.

On the second day, God separated the waters. Many think this is separating the water in the sky from the water on the ground. No, this is much more vast. We know this from reading verses 14,15, and 20. In verses 14 and 15, the firmament reaches into outer space. In verse 20, it speaks of breathable air, in the atmosphere where birds fly. Think about how big our God is since he created all that is, even before there were stars, planets, and moons. He made those spaces for them to fit before they existed.

On the third day, God created plants, trees, and all sorts of vegetation. Without trees, there would not be oxygen. All living things need oxygen. This was all part of the plan. Vegetation also is a form of food. Sheep need grass to eat. Fruit-bearing trees provide great sources of vitamins and more. If our Creator took such care in preparing a place for us before he created us, is this not a sign of His love for us?

Dear Lord Jesus,

Your Word shows us that You loved us first over and over again. It shows intense care and work in preparing the world for our existence. Yet, so many of us humans do not turn to You. Lord, change me so that I may be a better example of Your love. Then use me to show them Your love.

In Jesus name, Amen.

DAY #4
GENESIS 1:14-19

14 And God said, Let there be lights in the firmament of the heaven to divide the day from the night; and let them be for signs, and for seasons, and for days, and years:
15 And let them be for lights in the firmament of the heaven to give light upon the earth: and it was so.
16 And God made two great lights; the greater light to rule the day, and the lesser light to rule the night: *he made* the stars also.
17 And God set them in the firmament of the heaven to give light upon the earth,
18 And to rule over the day and over the night, and to divide the light from the darkness: and God saw that *it was* good.
19 And the evening and the morning were the fourth day.

This verse in truth negates the concept of the Big Bang Theory. On the fourth day not the first, the sun and the moon were created. Think about the planning that was involved in preparing for this creative moment, since it happened on the fourth day. What is interesting here is that on the third day, before there was a sun and moon, God created plant life. That means that plant life, all trees, and every form, were bathing in God's light before the creation of the sun.

God also created the stars, comets, and planets and comets that adorn the skies at night. Without those lights, we would have no comprehension of the vastness of God's power. The closest star is thought to be about 21 trillion miles from Earth. Yet our God set it there with a purpose. Space is seen by some as a new place to explore. My personal thoughts of stars are they are like clouds in that they are HIS paintings at night. Stars have been used for navigation for centuries. As the Earth orbits the sun, we see changes in the sky at night and new constellations every month. God set each star in its place with purpose.

Dear Lord Jesus,

You are so much greater than we can conceive or understand. The very idea, that you would show such love to us in the manner in which You created the earth and then us is beyond our comprehension. You painted a story of love in the creation story, just for us. Here you show us so well, that You first loved us. Lord, mold me into a better example of Your love so that I may be able to share that with others.

In Jesus name, Amen.

DAY #5
GENESIS 1:20-31

20 And God said, Let the waters bring forth abundantly the moving creature that has life, and fowl *that* may fly above the earth in the open firmament of heaven.
21 And God created great whales, and every living creature that moves, which the waters brought forth abundantly, after their kind, and every winged fowl after his kind: and God saw that *it was* good.
22 And God blessed them, saying, Be fruitful, and multiply, and fill the waters in the seas, and let fowl multiply in the earth.
23 And the evening and the morning were the fifth day.
24 And God said, Let the earth bring forth the living creature after his kind, cattle, and creeping thing, and beast of the earth after his kind: and it was so.
25 And God made the beast of the earth after his kind, and cattle after their kind, and every thing that creeps upon the earth after his kind: and God saw that *it was* good.
26 And God said, Let us make man in our image, after our likeness: and let them have dominion over the fish of the sea, and over the fowl of the air, and over the cattle, and over all the earth, and over every creeping thing that creeps upon the earth.
27 So God created man in his *own* image, in the image of God created he him; male and female created he them.
28 And God blessed them, and God said unto them, Be fruitful, and multiply, and replenish the earth, and subdue it:

29 And God said, Behold, I have given you every herb bearing seed, which *is* upon the face of all the earth, and every tree, in the which *is* the fruit of a tree yielding seed; to you it shall be for meat.

30 And to every beast of the earth, and to every fowl of the air, and to every thing that creeps upon the earth, wherein *there is* life, *I have given* every green herb for meat: and it was so.

31 And God saw every thing that he had made, and, behold, *it was* very good. And the evening and the morning were the sixth day.

There is an incredible beauty and perfection in the order in which God created the earth. Plant life came before fish, animals, insects, and humans so that there would be oxygen and food. This order making humans last is a display of God's omniscience. He knew the best order. There is so much wisdom in this order, scientists should marvel over it. Also surprising is that each living thing God created had the ability to reproduce. Then he blessed his work telling it to be fruitful and multiply.

The universal concepts of reproduction alone are amazing. The different ways God's creation perceives the world around them is mind-numbing. There is so much to be learned about God's love from the intricate designs he left on us. Not only did he make each one after their kind, he made each one individual.

Think about the importance of being treated not as a group, but being treated as an individual. Today we have laws protecting individual rights because they are GOD GIVEN. God loved us so

(continued from previous page)
and have dominion over the fish of the sea, and over the fowl of the air, and over every living thing that moves upon the earth.

much that he was concerned for who we were as individuals right at the beginning. This is love.

Dear Lord Jesus,

It never ceases to amaze me, that Your Word shows us from the beginning to the prophesied end of time, as we know it, how much You love us. You are truly a generous loving God, with a desire for us to also be this image of love. Lord, please continue to work on me teaching me to love.

In Jesus name, Amen.

DAY #6
GENESIS 2:1-3

1   Thus the heavens and the earth were finished, and all the host of them.
2   And on the seventh day God ended his work which he had made; and he rested on the seventh day from all his work which he had made.
3   And God blessed the seventh day, and sanctified it: because that in it he had rested from all his work which God created and made.

The importance of rest is given by God as an example to all mankind. God showed us in the beginning, in that first week when earth and all of creation came into being, that rest has its place in our lives. Those who ignore this important fact pay a horrible price either with their life, their health, or their family. Sometimes the effect comes in a trifecta of horrible realities as a punishment for ignoring something simple that was established at the beginning. Plain and simple, as often as it must be said, REST IS IMPORTANT!

When one works a farm it can seem as if there is never time to rest. This could be one of the reasons God created seasons. Seasons force farmers to take rests. Family businesses are often not effected by seasons today. Today, work is often done from home. Blending the concept of home life with business life. When this happens, there is a blur of how to organize time. What is important can be forgotten. People need to prioritize placing God first, family second, and business somewhere down the road from those two big priorities.

Today most countries have labor laws requiring a period of rest. In the USA and some other countries, lunchtime and 15-minute breaks are mandatory for most employees. Rest has to become a priority in our lives because God gave us that example.

However, that does not mean a rest from being a believer. If anything, it means this knowledge of where the importance of rest came from should be shared. Once again, in that first week, God shows his love for us by teaching us this important concept through HIS example.

Dear Lord Jesus,

It is an amazing thing that rest is an example of Your love. It is another example of You first loving us. Help us as foolish children wake up to what You have done, and what You are doing today, to see Your love in Your creation. Lord use us to be examples of that love.

In Jesus name, Amen.

DAY #7
GENESIS 2:4-7

4   These *are* the generations of the heavens and of the earth when they were created, in the day that the LORD God made the earth and the heavens,
5   And every plant of the field before it was in the earth, and every herb of the field before it grew: for the LORD God had not caused it to rain upon the earth, and *there was* not a man to till the ground.
6   But there went up a mist from the earth, and watered the whole face of the ground.
7   And the LORD God formed man *of* the dust of the ground, and breathed into his nostrils the breath of life; and man became a living soul.

Verse 4 starts with "these are the generations of the heavens and of the earth." This word choice is repeated eleven times in the book of Genesis. It speaks to giving fine details and usually speaks of descendants as those details. It is an introduction to the details of the creation story. It explains how plants could survive without rain. It also provides the details of man's creation. We are formed from the dust of the earth. Note that the word creation is not used here. In the Bible, create means to make from nothing (ex nihilo). God started with dust. Here the word form is used.

In these verses, we have the first usage of the "Lord God," which in Hebrew is "Yahweh Elohim." Matthew Henry, the Great commentator says this about the new name:

> "…a God of power and perfection, a finishing God. As we find him known by his name Jehovah when he appeared to perform what he had promised (Ex. 6:3), so now we have him known by that name, when he had perfected what he had begun. Jehovah is that great and incommunicable name of God which denotes his having his being of himself, and his giving being to all things; fitly therefore is he called by that name now that heaven and earth are finished."

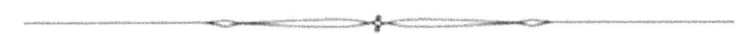

Dear Lord Jesus,

You are the God of power! You are the Alpha and the Omega. You are the one by whom all things were created. It is a message of love to tell us about our beginning. Just as adopted children wish to know their parents, we all want to have some clue about our beginnings. Lord, Thank you for the honor of sharing this with us. Thank you for teaching us about Your name. May you be glorified!

In Jesus name, Amen.

DAY #8
GENESIS 2:8-15

8   And the LORD God planted a garden eastward in Eden; and there he put the man whom he had formed.
9   And out of the ground made the LORD God to grow every tree that is pleasant to the sight, and good for food; the tree of life also in the midst of the garden, and the tree of knowledge of good and evil.
10 And a river went out of Eden to water the garden; and from there it was parted, and became into four heads.
11 The name of the first *is* Pison: that *is* it which compasses the whole land of Havilah, where *There is* gold;
12 And the gold of that land *is* good: there *is* bdellium and the onyx stone.
13 And the name of the second river *is* Gihon: the same *is* it that compassesthe whole land of Ethiopia.
14 And the name of the third river *is* Hiddekel: that *is* it which goes toward the east of Assyria. And the fourth river *is* Euphrates.
15 And the LORD God took the man, and put him into the garden of Eden to dress it and to keep it.

God who created man treated man like a treasure. He prepared a place for him. Think about where your earthly treasures are. Did you prepare the place where they are? When you think about this, you can compare it to a husband and wife preparing a room for the baby that is coming. They invest time and money and love making that space precious just for that child! God's garden, the garden of Eden can be seen like the crib, and the nursery is prepared for the child. It was a precious place. A place prepared with love, a place for man to grow. There are things placed just so, to help the child to grow and learn through play and more. How wonderful must the garden have been that God prepared? Man needs work also. God gave him a job on day 1, to care for the garden. Man needs the business of doing to feel content. He needs to accomplish tasks, reach out, and do something with effort. He needs the satisfaction of seeing his effort rewarded. There is an expectation that man is ready for this task. Some people think of Eden as a place of rest. It was a place of joy because it was a place man could work. He could put forth effort and see the fruit of his labor. God loved us so much he gave us what we needed to feel whole at the beginning!

Dear Lord Jesus,

You created a garden not an ivory house for Adam. You furnished it with nature better than today's works of art. You prepared the floor his bare feet walked on, the place he would rest, and more as a special treasure just for him. Lord, Your love for us is so precious. Help me to become one who shares that love. Work on me that my steps in life may be one that points others to see your love.

In Jesus name, Amen.

DAY #9
GENESIS 2:16-25

16   And the LORD God commanded the man, saying, Of every tree of the garden you may thou may freely eat:
17   But of the tree of the knowledge of good and evil, you shall not eat of it: for in the day that you eat thereof you shall surely die.
18   And the LORD God said, *It is* not good that the man should be alone; I will make him an help meet for him.
19   And out of the ground the LORD God formed every beast of the field, and every fowl of the air; and brought *them* unto Adam to see what he would call them: and whatsoever Adam called every living creature, that *was* the name thereof.
20   And Adam gave names to all cattle, and to the fowl of the air, and to every beast of the field; but for Adam there was not found an help meet for him.
21   And the LORD God caused a deep sleep to fall upon Adam, and he slept: and he took one of his ribs, and closed up the flesh instead thereof;
22   And the rib, which the LORD God had taken from man, made he a woman, and brought her unto the man.
23   And Adam said, This *is* now bone of my bones, and flesh of my flesh: she shall be called Woman, because she was taken out of Man.
24   Therefore shall a man leave his father and his mother, and shall cleave unto his wife: and they shall be one flesh.
25   And they were both naked, the man and his wife, and were not ashamed.

When you read chapter 1 of Genesis and then read 2:18-19, it looks like there is a change in the order of creation. In Genesis 1, God creates the animals and then creates man. In Genesis 2:18-19 it looks like the order is reversed. However, what many miss is that woman is yet to be created and she completes the creation of man. This is not a change in order. Chapter 2 gives a detailed account of man's creation, including the creation of male and female and their separate nature.

Verse 20 can be seen as God's sense of humor. He knew the sins of men before they were created. How is this humorous? When God created the living creatures, he created them male and female so they could reproduce and be fruitful. Today's fantasy literature has half-man-half-beast creatures. It is fantasy and no more. God's love for us is demonstrated here also. He tells us that we need to be with others. We cannot be an island unto ourselves. Better, he does not want us to be alone with just animals as best friends.

Men are simple creations of God that often miss what is right in front of them. We (men) need help. No creature comforts can help us with this. We can talk to our animal friends. We can train them to do incredible things, but they will never be equal partners with us. No matter what fantasy things are thought up by man, God set things straight in the first 2 chapters of HIS WORD on this. God created man and woman.

God made a woman from a part of man. That by itself lifts women up. God created her from Adam's rib. This is very important as it recognizes her role and importance to man. She was created according to this passage to be a helper. She is not a slave, she is not dumber than man. She is different. We as men need to celebrate that difference. Sometimes men like to announce they are lords of their own castles, demand their wives be nothing but servants, and be treated not as equals. Doing that ignores that in Genesis 1, God considered both male and female, "man" as a whole.

Dear Lord Jesus,

You know our sinful ways before we even start to go down the wrong path. You provide ways out of the depths of the darkness of sin, through the light of YOUR WORD. How is it that You plan for us to deal with our present reality thousands of years before the present came to be? Yet, this is another proof of Your love for us. Lord, please continue to work on me. Mold me into an example of Your love so others may see YOU instead of me.

In Jesus name, Amen.

DAY #10
GENESIS 2:21-3:5

21   And the LORD God caused a deep sleep to fall upon Adam, and he slept: and he took one of his ribs, and closed up the flesh instead thereof;
22   And the rib, which the LORD God had taken from man, made he a woman, and brought her unto the man.
23   And Adam said, This *is* now bone of my bones, and flesh of my flesh: she shall be called Woman, because she was taken out of Man.
24   Therefore shall a man leave his father and his mother, and shall cleave unto his wife: and they shall be one flesh.
25   And they were both naked, the man and his wife, and were not ashamed.

3:1	Now the serpent was more subtil than any beast of the field which the LORD God had made. And he said unto the woman, Yea, has God said, You shall not eat of every tree of the garden?
2	And the woman said unto the serpent, We may eat of the fruit of the trees of the garden:
3	But of the fruit of the tree which *is* in the midst of the garden, God has said, You shall not eat of it, neither shall You touch it, lest You die.
4	And the serpent said unto the woman, You shall not surely die:
5	For God does know that in the day You eat thereof, then your eyes shall be opened, and You shall be as gods, knowing good and evil.

    Eve, the woman, has now added to the word of God. God talked about eating NOT touching. However, with respect to avoiding temptation, Eve was right. Touching that which God says no to, is sinful in that you are willing to place temptation before yourself. Women think differently than men. Males marvel at how different the female brain is, and how it sees things differently than their own ability. But, the truth is that Eve added to God's Word, what she thought about what was said to her. Our own words do not have the everlasting importance, that God's words do. Adding to them is dangerous not only to ourselves but to those around us and those to come.

    Eve spoke of not touching. Did she obey that part? Was it because she knew she added that part, that placing this fruit in her hand was easier?

Dear Lord Jesus,

You watch over me, protect me, make me feel special, and listen to my prayers, even those just said in my head. You even answer my prayers! Lord, make me more like You. I want to be able to share this incredible love You have for me with others. Strengthen me. Embolden me. Place me where I can share your wonders.

In Jesus name, Amen.

DAY #11
GENESIS 3:6-7

6   And when the woman saw that the tree *was* good for food, and that it *was* pleasant to the eyes, and a tree to be desired to make *one* wise, she took of the fruit thereof, and did eat, and gave also unto her husband with her; and he did eat.
7   And the eyes of them both were opened, and they knew that they *were* naked; and they sewed fig leaves together, and made themselves aprons.

Yes, the woman gave the fruit to Adam. Yes, she sinned first but this was not a race was it? Nor is it a blame game! Grow up! Time to look at this like an adult. What happened to Adam is part of sinful nature. Sin separates us from God. It is possible that without Eve even knowing it, she felt the loneliness of being separated from God, and enticed Adam to join her to relieve that loneliness. The truth is that "enticement" or tempting others to join you in sin is never satisfying the gaping hole that was created by our sinful nature. Being tied to others in sin cannot be compared to being tied intimately to God. Adam and Eve had an incredibly intimate relationship with God before they sinned. They walked in the Garden with HIM. That means wherever they were, since they were always in the Garden of Eden, God was there with them. They communicated freely with God. It was normal! Only by eating that forbidden fruit did the idea that they could hide from God appear in their minds. It was silly, stupid, and delusional. Even the reasoning was that bad. So what they were naked! Had not God been there with them always as they had been – naked? God did not have a problem with it, why should they? This reasoning is the reasoning of a child when one is caught doing something bad.

Eve's sharing of the fruit and bringing Adam also into sin with her was part of sin nature. King Solomon wrote about this in Proverbs 1:10-14

> 10 My son, if sinners entice you, consent not.
> 11 If they say, Come with us, let us lay wait for blood, let us lurk privily for the innocent without cause:
> 12 Let us swallow them up alive as the grave; and whole, as those that go down into the pit:
> 13 We shall find all precious substance, we shall fill our houses with spoil:
> 14 Cast in your lot among us; let us all have one purse:

Sin nature desires company. It has the delusion this is to make them more powerful as a group. But the truth is, it is the desire to fill the whole left by being separated from God.

Hebrews 10:25 tells us as believers to not avoid gathering together in unity with our Christian brothers and sisters. The benefit here is not filling a whole left by the void of sin. The benefit is receiving encouragement in living on for Christ. You learn more about this great Saviour. When you worship together it is more powerful. When you pray together, there is Jesus also! How much greater is the gathering together of the saints, than the gathering of sinners!

Dear Lord Jesus,

I will never be able to comprehend how much love You have for us, that even in our gatherings as believers, You grant us such great blessings. Worship is better and, prayer is stronger with others. You love us so much that You gave us men to teach us more about You and Your love for us. As Your Word says, "(Your) mercies are new every morning." Praise You for them! Lord, please continue to work on me. Mold me more into someone who loves like You do so others may see You in me.

In Jesus name, Amen.

DAY #12
GENESIS 3:8-13

8   And they heard the voice of the LORD God walking in the garden in the cool of the day: and Adam and his wife hid themselves from the presence of the LORD God amongst the trees of the garden.

9   And the LORD God called unto Adam, and said unto him, Where *are* you?

10	And he said, I heard your voice in the garden, and I was afraid, because I *was* naked; and I hid myself.
11	And he said, Who told you that you *were* naked? Have you eaten of the tree, of whereof I commanded you that you should not eat?
12	And the man said, The woman whom you gave *to be* with me, she gave me of the tree, and I did eat.
13	And the LORD God said unto the woman, What *is* this *that you have* done? And the woman said, The serpent beguiled me, and I did eat.

Sometimes when this passage is read you want to ask more questions than you find answers. Why did Eve not question when the snake talked? Why was there no questioning of the claimed knowledge of the snake? No matter how many questions run through your head about this event, the answers come down to the state of innocence of mankind being one of implicit trust There was never a reason not to trust before. No need to question anything that existed because that would require a sense of right and wrong.

Add to this that God so frequently walked through the garden with Adam and Eve that you wonder how they felt they could hide from God. That sadly is easily answered. Because sin separates man from God. It makes man stink and marks him as a foul creature. This horrible aspect of sin creates the belief that man can actually find someplace to hide, into whatever holds a person finds, that spot can be safe from God, while at the same time knowing it must be a lie.

How did God handle the separation? Did He come angrily? Did He raise His voice? No. He simply asked, "Where are you?" God called man back to Himself by asking questions, which made man answer and talk to Him. God wants this relationship with us. This is the love we cannot understand. Even when man first became sinful, God sought out man and wanted to bridge the gap. He listened to the foolish answers. He listened to the blame game. But even before that, he allowed time to think over what wrong had been done. HE, GOD, gave the man a chance to repent from the wrong. Yet, that did not happen.

Dear Lord Jesus,

How is it that You love us so much? Even from our creation, You loved us. Lord, there is nothing we have done to earn or deserve any of this. Lord, please make me more into someone who is an example of Your love.

In Jesus name, Amen.

DAY #13
GENESIS 3:14-19

14 And the LORD God said unto the serpent, Because you hast done this, you *are* cursed above all cattle, and above every beast of the field; upon your belly shalt you go, and dust shalt you eat all the days of your life:
15 And I will put enmity between you and the woman, and between your seed and her seed; it shall bruise your head, and you shalt bruise his heel.

16   Unto the woman he said, I will greatly multiply your sorrow and your conception; in sorrow you shalt bring forth children; and your desire *shall be* to your husband, and he shall rule over you.

17   And unto Adam he said, Because you have hearkened unto the voice of your wife, and have eaten of the tree, of which I commanded you, saying, You shall not eat of it: cursed *is* the ground for your sake; in sorrow shall you eat *of* it all the days of your life;

18   Thorns also and thistles shall it bring forth to thee; and you shall eat the herb of the field;

19   In the sweat of your face shalt you eat bread, till you return unto the ground; for out of it you were taken: for dust you *are*, and unto dust shalt you return.

There are three groups cursed here: all snakes, all women, and all men. But God did not just pass judgement on us here. He also gave us a way out of this mess through a messianic prophecy, which would take us a long time to grasp.

In this punishment, God tells each one why they are being punished and then what the punishment is. In each of the judgements/curses on men and women, there is a blessing. Women experience pain in child birth as a result of this curse. Today we know that where there is strong emotion, there are strong memories. Then the woman is put under the husband. This wording is actually important. It declares order to a marriage. Some may think this a curse, but order organizes. It allows for clear thought and frees us in other ways. Note that this order is within the confines not of everything but in marriage. This in many ways makes God the first supporter of women having equal rights.

Men are cursed to work. They are told that their work will not always benefit them. Work is something that Adam was given in the garden of Eden before the fall. Strangely, this means work is a blessing and a need for us. Yet no one likes working to accomplish nothing. Few are okay with earning nothing through work. There are sayings, that come from this curse. "Nothing worth doing comes easily." Here again we have God showing His love to us, even in the judgement of our sin.

Dear Lord Jesus,

How is it that even when you judge us, you bless us. Your mercies are indeed new every morning. We here the creation story and hurl blame at Adam and Eve for making a dumb mistake, and rarely thank You, for Your mercy and blessings. Lord God, help me to see as You do. Help me to see the promise in each and every person. Help me to show others this love You have for us. I want others to be freed from the bondage of sin into the freeness of Your love.

In Jesus love, Amen.

DAY #14
GENESIS 3:20-24

20 And Adam called his wife's name Eve; because she was the mother of all living.
21 Unto Adam also and to his wife did the LORD God make coats of skins, and clothed them.

22 And the LORD God said, Behold, the man is become as one of us, to know good and evil: and now, lest he put forth his hand, and take also of the tree of life, and eat, and live for ever:
23 Therefore the LORD God sent him forth from the garden of Eden, to till the ground from whence he was taken.
24 So he drove out the man; and he placed at the east of the garden of Eden Cherubims, and a flaming sword which turned every way, to keep the way of the tree of life.

It is only since DNA showed one common ancestor of all mankind, that the story of Adam Eve is now more than just a Bible story. Science now testifies to their being only one set of parents to start things off. This negates evolution, the random shot in the dark at something becoming real.

Verse 21, speaks volumes more than the 18-word sentence states. Man cannot cover his sin on his own. That will only result in failure. God clothed them in animal skins. That means at the least one or two animals were sacrificed for God to provide them with clothing. It is believed that the animal was a lamb. This would explain Abel keeping sheep in the next chapter and his knowledge of the sacrifice as being something taught by his parents who received the gift of clothing, a cover of their sin of nakedness from God almighty. "Without the shedding of blood there is no remission of sins" (Hebrews 9:22). With this sacrifice their sins were forgiven. God provided a way back to HIM! He gave Adam and Eve the ability to atone for their sins. But it was only a covering. This was a sign of something better coming. Something that would pay the full price for sin. Something that would wash away the stench of sin and not simply cover it. That something being the blood of Jesus shed for us on the cross.

Now the Garden of Eden containing the tree of life became hidden to man. But today because of Jesus being the perfect sacrifice for our sins, we have access to something better, which is a one way ticket to paradise with God. It is simply faith in HIM and what he did on the cross.

Dear Lord Jesus,

Thank you for setting things in motion from the beginning for your salvation. This shows me you cared for ne long before I even grasped a thought. Your love is so deep and plans so far ahead of my needs. Lord, how is it You love us so? Lord work on me. I need to be the better example of your love.

In Jesus name, Amen.

DAY #15
GENESIS 4:1-10

1   And Adam knew Eve his wife; and she conceived, and bare Cain, and said, I have gotten a man from the LORD.
2   And she again bare his brother Abel. And Abel was a keeper of sheep, but Cain was a tiller of the ground.
3   And in process of time it came to pass, that Cain brought of the fruit of the ground an offering unto the LORD.
4   And Abel, he also brought of the firstlings of his flock and of the fat thereof. And the LORD had respect unto Abel and to his offering:

5	But unto Cain and to his offering he had not respect. And Cain was very wroth, and his countenance fell.
6	And the LORD said unto Cain, Why are you angry? and why is your countenance fallen?
7	If you do well, shall you not be accepted? and if you do not well, sin lies at the door. And unto you *shall be* his desire, and you shall rule over him.
8	And Cain talked with Abel his brother: and it came to pass, when they were in the field, that Cain rose up against Abel his brother, and slew him.
9	And the LORD said unto Cain, Where *is* Abel your brother? And he said, I know not: *Am* I my brother's keeper?
10	And he said, What have you done? the voice of your brother's blood cries unto me from the ground.

Look at what this passage says about Abel's offering. Abel brought out of the first of his flock as an offering. Now look at Cain's offering. It is not said that his offering was of the first fruits of the harvest. Cain thought himself more worthy of those first fruits. He made that offering to himself. When it came to placing an offering before God, Abel honored God with what he brought, and his heart was in the right place. Cain skimped on what he offered, and his heart was in the wrong place. He was jealous only because Abel was blessed with respect and he was not. Here we have the first example of sibling rivalry and … murder.

Cain was arrogant! When God approached him, not to accuse him, but to get an admission of wrongdoing. Cain believed he could deceive God. He thought himself smarter than God and responded with sarcasm, saying "am I my brother's keeper?" Adam had tried to side-step the issue and use the blame game when he sinned. But his son Cain tried to pretend there was nothing wrong! He tried using the innocent look. But as expected he could not fool God.

How often do we try to get out of the sins we do? How often do we try to hide and pretend that we didn't do it? As Christians, we are supposed to be better than this. As believers, we need to admit to and beg forgiveness for our sins. We can never be perfect like Jesus. But we should own our own mistakes and purposeful errors.

Dear Lord Jesus,

I am but a fool who somehow stumbled into Your love. You loved me first. You love us before we even grasp who You are. How is it that You love me when I am so often doing what is wrong? Lord, mold me and make me into someone who loves like You do. I want to be so much better than I am. Mold me, Lord.

In Jesus' name, Amen.

DAY #16
GENESIS 4:11-16

11   And now *are* you cursed from the earth, which has opened her mouth to receive your brother's blood from your hand;

12   When you till the ground, it shall not henceforth yield unto you her strength; a fugitive and a vagabond shall you be in the earth.

13   And Cain said unto the LORD, My punishment *is* greater than I can bear.

14   Behold, you have driven me out this day from the face of the earth; and from your face shall I be hid; and I shall be a fugitive and a vagabond in the earth; and it shall come to pass, *that* every one that finds me shall slay me.
15   And the LORD said unto him, Therefore whosoever slays Cain, vengeance shall be taken on him sevenfold. And the LORD set a mark upon Cain, lest any finding him should kill him.
16   And Cain went out from the presence of the LORD, and dwelt in the land of Nod, on the east of Eden.

Cain twists the Word of God like a compulsive liar, saying, "Behold, you have driven me out this day from the face of the earth; and from your face shall I be hid; and I shall be a fugitive and a vagabond in the earth; and it shall come to pass, *that* every one that finds me shall slay me." Cain sounds like an "attention hog." All he can think about is "poor me." Not once does he say those three important words, "I have sinned." "Nor does he say, "I was wrong." Instead, he adds to what God said. This may be something he learned from his mother since we know she did that too. Cain was not "driven from the face of the earth," nor was he "hid from God's face." This sounds a lot like what Adam and Eve thought when they sinned, that they could hide from God.

Cain's flair for drama and attention, has him adding more wild statements, about there being others who will kill him. According to what the Bible shows here, there are only three people on earth: Adam, Eve, and Cain, because Cain had killed his brother. These other people Cain speaks of are not only imaginary at this point. Cain, the murderer, says this in an attempt to get a lighter sentence. But that does not happen. Instead, an additional punishment of a mark is made on Cain.

Dear Lord Jesus,

You took care and attempted to bring even the first murderer, Cain to repentance by talking with him. Yet he never admitted his sin, only acknowledged his punishment. Lord, work on me that I may not make excuses for my actions. Lord, I am but a sinner. I am shamefully aware of it. Lord, please forgive me. Help me Lord, to ask forgiveness of those I have wronged. Help me to be an example of a changed heart, that found You. Lord, let others see Your work in me that YOU have done.

In Jesus name, Amen.

DAY #17
GENESIS 4:17-24

17   And Cain knew his wife; and she conceived, and bare Enoch: and he built a city, and called the name of the city, after the name of his son, Enoch.
18   And unto Enoch was born Irad: and Irad begat Mehujael: and Mehujael begat Methusael: and Methusael begat Lamech.
19   And Lamech took unto him two wives: the name of the one *was* Adah, and the name of the other Zillah.
20   And Adah bare Jabal: he was the father of such as dwell in tents, and *of such as have* cattle.
21   And his brother's name *was* Jubal: he was the father of all such as handle the harp and organ.

22   And Zillah, she also bare Tubalcain, an instructor of every artificer in brass and iron: and the sister of Tubalcain *was* Naamah.
23   And Lamech said unto his wives, Adah and Zillah, Hear my voice; you wives of Lamech, listen unto my speech: for I have slain a man to my wounding, and a young man to my hurt.
24   If Cain shall be avenged sevenfold, truly Lamech seventy and sevenfold.

Cain has children and grandchildren, this is evidence that God kept his part of the agreement. But, if Cain never repented, did he pass down the blame game to his descendants? Lamech kills someone also. Think about this Cain killed his brother. Who did Lamech kill? Was it not a cousin, an uncle, or a nephew? There is no expectation of a punishment, partly because Cain's children have no idea what Cain lost. There is nothing holding them back from committing the vilest sins, even in the sin of murder Lamech sees it as wrong, but does not repent, instead he expects God to protect him more than his father. The children of Cain are shortening their family line. Murder is ok, so what isn't ok? Not exactly the family you want living next door to you. What happens when you put a bunch of people together who feel murder is OK, rape, robbery, etc. are nothing. This is why you do not hear about Cain's descendants again.

Dear Lord Jesus,

You told us that thinking of committing a sin is just as bad as committing a sin. Lord, work on me. Purify my thoughts. Remove any anger I feel. Remove those distractions from me that would put me on a wrong way of thinking. Lord, I need to be more like You! I want to share Your love, not my own foolishness. Lord, remove whatever vanities, whatever foolishness from myself that You alone may be glorified.

In Jesus name, Amen.

DAY #18
GENESIS 4:25-26

25 And Adam knew his wife again; and she bare a son, and called his name Seth: For God, *said she*, has appointed me another seed instead of Abel, whom Cain slew.
26 And to Seth, to him also there was born a son; and he called his name Enos: then began men to call upon the name of the LORD.

Adam and Eve did not have another child until Cain killed Abel. Maybe they found their hands full raising the two of them. Just look at how differently Seth raised his own children. When Enos comes, then men begin to call on the Lord. This tells us two things. 1. Adam and Eve and their children began to neglect God, somewhere after Abel and Cain were born. 2. After Enos was born, they started to rebuild their relationship with God.

One of the foolish things we do is to allow distractions to take away our time with God. If devotions are a morning routine for you, suddenly, there are a whole bunch of distractions at that time.

We have to tell ourselves what is true about our relationship with God. When we pay more attention to HIM, our lives are better! It goes even deeper. When we raise our children while seeking God, our children's lives are better and this passes down! We have to fight the distractions that try to keep us from the God who loves us. He is always there trying to maintain the relationship. It is us who let things slide.

Dear Lord Jesus,

Help me to be better at loving You. Lord, help me to simply say no to the distractions in my life. Help me to stand up and shut the door on the things that take my time from being spent with You. Lord, my time with you makes me a better person. I know this. Lord, keep pounding that into me. I want to be an example of Your love. I may not know how. But it is something I need to be not for me but to share Your love which I don't deserve.

In Jesus name, Amen.

DAY #19
GENESIS 5:1-24

1   This *is* the book of the generations of Adam. In the day that God created man, in the likeness of God made he him;
2   Male and female created he them; and blessed them, and called their name Adam, in the day when they were created.

3 And Adam lived an hundred and thirty years, and begat *a son* in his own likeness, after his image; and called his name Seth:
4 And the days of Adam after he had begotten Seth were eight hundred years: and he begat sons and daughters:
5 And all the days that Adam lived were nine hundred and thirty years: and he died.
6 And Seth lived an hundred and five years, and begat Enos:
7 And Seth lived after he begat Enos eight hundred and seven years, and begat sons and daughters:
8 And all the days of Seth were nine hundred and twelve years: and he died.
9 And Enos lived ninety years, and begat Cainan:
10 And Enos lived after he begat Cainan eight hundred and fifteen years, and begat sons and daughters:
11 And all the days of Enos were nine hundred and five years: and he died.
12 And Cainan lived seventy years, and begat Mahalaleel:
13 And Cainan lived after he begat Mahalaleel eight hundred and forty years, and begat sons and daughters:
14 And all the days of Cainan were nine hundred and ten years: and he died.
15 And Mahalaleel lived sixty and five years, and begat Jared:
16 And Mahalaleel lived after he begat Jared eight hundred and thirty years, and begat sons and daughters:
17 And all the days of Mahalaleel were eight hundred ninety and five years: and he died.
18 And Jared lived an hundred sixty and two years, and he begat Enoch:
19 And Jared lived after he begat Enoch eight hundred years, and begat sons and daughters:
20 And all the days of Jared were nine hundred sixty and two years: and he died.

21   And Enoch lived sixty and five years, and begat Methuselah:
22   And Enoch walked with God after he begat Methuselah three hundred years, and begat sons and daughters:
23   And all the days of Enoch were three hundred sixty and five years:
24   And Enoch walked with God: and he *was* not; for God took him.

This genealogy begins a tradition of naming the firstborn son and not the others. This might be because from Adam on through this first generational list they had so many children. Seth is listed as the firstborn here. Adam and Eve lost not only Abel that day, they also lost Cain. This shows that they mourned the loss of both. When Enos was born man began to call on God. Somewhere in this genealogy, man starts to understand the importance of time with God.

Enoch becomes so close with God, that God takes him after three hundred and sixty-five years on the earth. What do you think his children learned if he had a great relationship with God? Enoch was just a sinful man like us. Yet, even before the birth of Christ, and before one book of the Bible was written to help guide the way, Enoch had such a beautiful relationship with God, that "he was taken." There are no imaginary aliens who did this, no imaginary place that he went to. These words communicate no sense of loss but of one rewarded for doing what is right. Enoch went to live with the CREATOR! He was rewarded for getting the importance of God in his life. Enoch had been married and had a lot of children, whom he taught about God. His firstborn being Methuselah who lived the longest of any human. Enoch was also the great-grandfather of Noah. What a legacy to leave behind. Enoch who loved God, taught this to his children. He taught the importance of separating yourself from the world. He taught the importance of setting time aside to be with God. Sadly, this communicates another truth. We as parents can lead a child on the path they should follow to God. But it is up to the child to choose to follow that path. No one can force them.

Dear Lord Jesus,

Who am I but one who desires to serve You? I want to be the parent who passes this love of You to my children. It hurts knowing I can't make choices for them as they grow older. That makes me wonder what You think of so many of my own foolish choices. Lord, change me. Make me into someone whose life shines only because of You. Let my life be one that glorifies You and points others to Your waiting arms of love.

In Jesus name, Amen.

DAY #20
GENESIS 5:25-32

25 And Methuselah lived an hundred eighty and seven years, and begat Lamech:
26 And Methuselah lived after he begat Lamech seven hundred eighty and two years, and begat sons and daughters:
27 And all the days of Methuselah were nine hundred sixty and nine years: and he died.

28	And Lamech lived an hundred eighty and two years, and begat a son:
29	And he called his name Noah, saying, This *same* shall comfort us concerning our work and toil of our hands, because of the ground which the LORD has cursed.
30	And Lamech lived after he begat Noah five hundred ninety and five years, and begat sons and daughters:
31	And all the days of Lamech were seven hundred seventy and seven years: and he died.
32	And Noah was five hundred years old: and Noah begat Shem, Ham, and Japheth.

ou have to wonder what was going on in this time period where men did not have children until they were over 100 years old! Today this would be laughed at in the medical community. But, they forget many things that make this possible. The earth was covered by a canopy of clouds, which would also influence the aging process. It does not say that these men did not have wives when they were young. This world was different.

Lamech gave his son the name "Noah." Noah means "rest." Matthew Henry, the great Commentator said his name:

> "… denotes not only the desire and expectation which parents generally have concerning their children (that, when they grow up, they will be comforts to them and helpers in their business, though they often prove otherwise) but an apprehension and prospect of something more. Very probably there were some prophecies that went before of him, as a person that should be wonderfully serviceable to his generation, which they so understood as to conclude that he was the promised seed…"

The listing here of Noah's children is also important and often overlooked. Japheth is the oldest but is listed last. Shem however is the child of promise through which Abraham, King David, and the Messiah come to us; and is listed first. Japheth was skipped over. This is an example of how God there is no distinction between races. Shem was Asian and listed first. Ham was black and listed second. Japheth was white, he was listed last. All three races came from the same Mom and Dad! Yet, another example of God's love.

Dear Lord Jesus,

What is it that causes men to not see Your love but the foolish blinders they put on themselves? You are the God who loves us so. You love us beyond anything we can comprehend. Even at the beginning, Your love was demonstrated to us over and over! Change me, Lord. Make me into one whose love is known not because of me, but because of what You have done in me!

In Jesus name, Amen.

DAY #21
GENESIS 6:1-12

1 And it came to pass, when men began to multiply on the face of the earth, and daughters were born unto them,
2 That the sons of God saw the daughters of men that they *were* fair; and they took them wives of all which they chose.

3   And the LORD said, My spirit shall not always strive with man, for that he also *is* flesh: yet his days shall be an hundred and twenty years.
4   There were giants in the earth in those days; and also after that, when the sons of God came in unto the daughters of men, and they bare *children* to them, the same *became* mighty men which *were* of old, men of renown.
5   And GOD saw that the wickedness of man *was* great in the earth, and *that* every imagination of the thoughts of his heart *was* only evil continually.
6   And it repented the LORD that he had made man on the earth, and it grieved him at his heart.
7   And the LORD said, I will destroy man whom I have created from the face of the earth; both man, and beast, and the creeping thing, and the fowls of the air; for it repents me that I have made them.
8   But Noah found grace in the eyes of the LORD.
9   These *are* the generations of Noah: Noah was a just man *and* perfect in his generations, *and* Noah walked with God.
10 And Noah begat three sons, Shem, Ham, and Japheth.
11 The earth also was corrupt before God, and the earth was filled with violence.
12 And God looked upon the earth, and, behold, it was corrupt; for all flesh had corrupted his way upon the earth.

The earth had become filled with creatures that were perversions of what God created because fallen angels had come and engaged in sexual activity with women. Noah found grace in God's eyes. That means Noah must have been listening to his father and grandfather. These two men who recognized the evils of their own time chose their wives carefully. They were pure and uncorrupted of the fallen angels. Noah is spoken of as a "just man perfect in his generations." This is not said of anyone else. Joseph, our Lord Jesus' stepfather on this earth, was called a just man in Matthew 1:9. What qualities did Noah have that God chose him? Looking at what a just man is in Proverbs and Ecclesiastes, says a lot.

> "Give *instruction* to a wise *man*, and he will be yet wiser: teach a just *man*, and he will increase in learning." (Pro 9:9)

> "The just *man* walks in his integrity: his children *are* blessed after him." (Pro 20:7)

> "For a just *man* falls seven times, and rises up again: but the wicked shall fall into mischief." (Pro 24:16)

> "For *there is* not a just man upon earth, that does good, and sins not. (Ecc 7:20)

Dear Lord Jesus,

Help me to not walk like a mouse but like a lion sharing the wonders of Your Word. Strengthen me, Lord. Push me not to skip my time with You. Encourage me to go beyond what I know and to stretch into a new understanding of Your Word! Lord, work on me.

In Jesus name, Amen.

DAY #22
GENESIS 6:13-22

13   And God said unto Noah, The end of all flesh is come before me; for the earth is filled with violence through them; and, behold, I will destroy them with the earth.

14   Make you an ark of gopher wood; rooms shall you make in the ark, and shall pitch it within and without with pitch.

15   And this *is the fashion* which you shall make it *of*: The length of the ark *shall be* three hundred cubits, the breadth of it fifty cubits, and the height of it thirty cubits.

16   A window shall you make to the ark, and in a cubit shall you finish it above; and the door of the ark shall you set in the side thereof; *with* lower, second, and third *stories* shall you make it.

17   And, behold, I, even I, do bring a flood of waters upon the earth, to destroy all flesh, wherein *is* the breath of life, from under heaven; *and* every thing that *is* in the earth shall die.

18   But with you will I establish my covenant; and you shall come into the ark, you, and your sons, and your wife, and your sons' wives with you.

19   And of every living thing of all flesh, two of every *sort* shall you bring into the ark, to keep *them* alive with you; they shall be male and female.

20   Of fowls after their kind, and of cattle after their kind, of every creeping thing of the earth after his kind, two of every *sort* shall come unto you, to keep *them* alive.

21   And take you unto you of all food that is eaten, and you shall gather *it* to you; and it shall be for food for you, and for them.

22   Thus did Noah; according to all that God commanded him, so did he.

God tells Noah, that he will "destroy them all with the earth." Here it is important to pay attention to detail. Noah was being told he, and his family were being excluded from destruction. God had something special in mind for them. Then comes the instructions on how to build the ark. This should have been an oddity that earned Noah and his family a lot of mockery. No one had seen a boat, much less something of this size. Add onto this that God told Noah, how he would "destroy them with the earth," with a massive flood. A world cataclysmic flood.

As Noah and his sons built the ark, the community had to take notice of the increased animal movement leading to Noah and his family. II Peter 2:5 tells us that Noah preached to "them" of righteousness. Noah believed he served the God of love. If they would but turn to God they would be saved. Sadly, Noah and his family built that ark and tended the animals alone. Not one of those Noah preached too, made a choice to love God. As a result, they chose their own deaths.

Today, Christians are to share the good news of Jesus with all. We are simply to share. We are not out there to debate, or to argue, but to share the message of hope found in Christ Jesus. It is not our responsibility to lead them to Christ. It is our responsibility to show them the way. It is all up to those who hear the message to make that choice for Christ. God reaps the harvest. We are simply to plant seeds.

Noah saw not one convert to his preaching. Noah's message of hope was all in an ark. Our message of hope is based on Jesus, God incarnate, offering Himself as a sacrifice for our sins. A truly perfect sacrifice for an imperfect people to grant the blessing of eternal life to those who choose to say, "Yes! I believe in You, Jesus!" Do we dare to be silent about such an important message?

Dear Lord Jesus,

You offer us so much. You gave us salvation through your sacrifice. You gave us Your Word, the Bible so that we can learn better how to seek You and follow You! Each day Your mercies are new. We can expect new and great thanks each day, because of You! Lord, help me to see that greatness. Help me to be like Noah, in always sharing the promise of hope in God. Use me to be that pointer to You.

In Jesus name, Amen.

DAY #23
GENESIS 7:1-9

1   And the LORD said unto Noah, Come you and all your house into the ark; for you have I seen righteous before me in this generation.
2   Of every clean beast you shall take to you by sevens, the male and his female: and of beasts that *are* not clean by two, the male and his female.
3   Of fowls also of the air by sevens, the male and the female; to keep seed alive upon the face of all the earth.
4   For yet seven days, and I will cause it to rain upon the earth forty days and forty nights; and every living substance that I have made will I destroy from off the face of the earth.
5   And Noah did according unto all that the LORD commanded him.

6   And Noah *was* six hundred years old when the flood of waters was upon the earth.

7   And Noah went in, and his sons, and his wife, and his sons' wives with him, into the ark, because of the waters of the flood.

8   Of clean beasts, and of beasts that *are* not clean, and of fowls, and of every thing that creeps upon the earth,

9   There went in two and two unto Noah into the ark, the male and the female, as God had commanded Noah.

Noah has finished building the ark with his sons. Noah, the man who heard the voice of God; the man whose sons trusted and believed in him when he said, "God told me to build an ark. We are going to have a flood." This small family that expanded from two to five, and then to eight took care of the animals, fed them, and more before they boarded the ark as well.

It was time. Ringing a bell to call the family for dinner, would not have raised a sense of urgency like this small conversation between God and Noah. It's TIME! Get the clean animals on in seven sets both male and female. The unclean in sets of two. Even the birds came in sets of seven. It was time! Get on the ark. We only have seven days before the rain starts! Noah had been preaching righteousness. Asking those who heard to repent and turn to God. Can you imagine the laughs and jeers when Noah and his family finally board the ark? Especially, with the size of the door. How would they ever close it? Rainwater from the sky. Today it is something seen as a normal part of weather. But then – rain fell for the first time. All that laughter at Noah's preaching came to a screeching halt. Laughter about his warning of rain stopped. But they laughed at the rain, believing it could not result in a flood. What would they think in a few days? The next week? The next month would be too late. We need a sense of urgency in our being to reach out to those who do not know Christ. We cannot know when their last day on earth is coming. It could be this very day. Would you rather be like Noah, having preached of doom and none listened, or be the one who held his/her tongue and watched their demise? The time is at hand.

Dear Lord Jesus,

Help me to be stronger. Help me to stand up and shout from the mountaintops that YOU ALONE ARE GOD! Lord, strengthen me that I may also strengthen others. Lord make my voice bolder. Put me in places where I can share your love with others. Lord, use me.

In Jesus name, Amen.

DAY #24
GENESIS 7:10-16

10   And it came to pass after seven days, that the waters of the flood were upon the earth.
11   In the six hundredth year of Noah's life, in the second month, the seventeenth day of the month, the same day were all the fountains of the great deep broken up, and the windows of heaven were opened.
12   And the rain was upon the earth forty days and forty nights.

13 In the selfsame day entered Noah, and Shem, and Ham, and Japheth, the sons of Noah, and Noah's wife, and the three wives of his sons with them, into the ark;
14 They, and every beast after his kind, and all the cattle after their kind, and every creeping thing that creeps upon the earth after his kind, and every fowl after his kind, every bird of every sort.
15 And they went in unto Noah into the ark, two and two of all flesh, wherein *is* the breath of life.
16 And they that went in, went in male and female of all flesh, as God had commanded him: and the LORD shut him in.

Sometimes in life, we get mad feeling like we thought we were doing what God wanted, but something now seems bad. God warned Noah that he was sending a flood, He told Noah to build the ark. Noah did that. He told Noah to get the animals and his family on the ark. Noah did that. But—Noah could not close the door! Can you imagine seeing the coming flood and having to wait for someone to close the ark door? Only God could close that door and you have to wait? The truth is that God did close that door! When God leads the way, jump through those open doors! When troubles come trust God to take care of things He has not given you the ability to handle. God closed the door to the ark that day and even made a watertight seal because Noah and his family listened to Him and believed!

Some of you may be engineers, thinking of ways Noah may have been able to close that door. But this was something God did. It was like HIS stamp of approval. HIS seal of all that was right in the little ark, compared to everything else dealing with the roaring flood waters. This was the one place touched by God!

Dear Lord Jesus,

We often do stupid things and Your love grabs hold of us and drags us back from whatever way we choose to stray. Lord, You know us better. You love us better. Help us to become a people who love You better through our words and deeds. Help us to shine in ways that show Your glory! We don't need praise. We need YOU lifted higher! Lord use us!

In Jesus name, Amen.

DAY #25
GENESIS 7:17-24

17   And the flood was forty days upon the earth; and the waters increased, and bare up the ark, and it was lifted up above the earth.
18   And the waters prevailed, and were increased greatly upon the earth; and the ark went upon the face of the waters.
19   And the waters prevailed exceedingly upon the earth; and all the high hills, that *were* under the whole heaven, were covered.
20   Fifteen cubits upward did the waters prevail; and the mountains were covered.
21   And all flesh died that moved upon the earth, both of fowl, and of cattle, and of beast, and of every creeping thing that creeps upon the earth, and every man:
22   All in whose nostrils *was* the breath of life, of all that *was* in the dry *land*, died.

23   And every living substance was destroyed which was upon the face of the ground, both man, and cattle, and the creeping things, and the fowl of the heaven; and they were destroyed from the earth: and Noah only remained *alive*, and they that *were* with him in the ark.

24   And the waters prevailed upon the earth an hundred and fifty days.

This sounds awful it was the death of all living things…except those – on the ark. God chose Noah and his family. Noah preached righteousness endlessly until he was told to get on the ark. He probably preached to those who could hear until God closed the door.

Closed doors protect those inside. They also say to those who recognize them, "no going back." With God closing the door of the ark. He sealed that door making it secure from leaks. There is more. God preserved those on the ark. Noah was told of the flood. He was told of the destruction to come. Noah was not told how long to prepare to live on the ark. That makes you wonder what kind of storage was needed for food for them and the animals. At a bare minimum 150 days' worth of food! Yet, it is also possible God provided their food. This type of miracle is seen in the Bible later. God's provision then, was our salvation. For without that provision of the ark and the food necessary to survive none of us today would be here. God saved Noah and his family and all the animals, insects, and birds on one ark. God's provision, went beyond saving them in an ark. It went beyond providing food for them. This was HIS shelter. It was HIS place of grace for them at that time. In God's arms, we flourish. We grow! We feel HIS presence and do not wonder if HE hears us! 150 days spent in HIS shelter. What would that have been like? The seas could have been rough outside. People can get tired of each other when in an enclosed space.

But when God is added to that mix …. The words safety and security become like a blanket held snugly about you.

Dear Lord Jesus,

How is it that You love us fools so much? What have we ever done to deserve Your love? Your Word from the beginning, proclaims such love to us, that we must be fools to deny it. Lord, help me to seek you more and more each day. Help me to be someone who sees Your love where others do not. Use me to share that love! Use me, Lord, that others may find You.

In Jesus name, Amen.

DAY #26
GENESIS 8:1-5

1   And God remembered Noah, and every living thing, and all the cattle that *was* with him in the ark: and God made a wind to pass over the earth, and the waters asswaged;
2   The fountains also of the deep and the windows of heaven were stopped, and the rain from heaven was restrained;
3   And the waters returned from off the earth continually: and after the end of the hundred and fifty days the waters were abated.
4   And the ark rested in the seventh month, on the seventeenth day of the month, upon the mountains of Ararat.

5 And the waters decreased continually until the tenth month: in the tenth *month*, on the first *day* of the month, were the tops of the mountains seen.

How would you feel even though you got in an ark God told you to build and that all but you, your family, and all the other living things on the boat are gone, and you have been on the boat for at least SEVEN MONTHS? Would you be wondering if God played some cruel cosmic joke on you? Would you be thinking, "God forgot about us?" Seven months at sea on the first boat recorded by all mankind, with no end in sight and then a jerking stuck feeling. Would you even know what it meant at first? Only one window. You stay another three months, and all you get to see are the mountain tops from that window. But it's a sign of hope. At least, at least the waters are going down. Still through that window, all they can see still isn't promising. Would you feel forgotten? Would you be wondering when does this ride end? Would you be going mad just wanting to get off?

All of these feelings were probably all too real for Noah and his family. Yet each little step was noticed as God remembering Noah! See, GOD DID NOT FORGET!

Then a rush of expectancy like an expectant father and mother would become like a rush insanely pushing on you making you think, "What has God got waiting for me when he does open that door?"

Dear Lord Jesus,

You close and open doors for us. Sometimes we sit and cry when doors get closed. Sometimes we lose all sense of hope when that door closes. But that open door we have to remember is YOUR plan! Help us Lord, to see Your hand in our lives. Help us to see where You want us to be and how important the little things we do can impact others. Lord, help us to see life ahead as waiting for the next wonder behind the next door You will open as being something wonderful beyond our expectations.

In Jesus name, Amen.

DAY #27
GENESIS 8:6-13

6   And it came to pass at the end of forty days, that Noah opened the window of the ark which he had made:

7   And he sent forth a raven, which went forth to and fro, until the waters were dried up from off the earth.

8   Also he sent forth a dove from him, to see if the waters were abated from off the face of the ground;

9   But the dove found no rest for the sole of her foot, and she returned unto him into the ark, for the waters *were* on the face of the whole earth: then he put forth his hand, and took her, and pulled her in unto him into the ark.

10   And he stayed yet other seven days; and again he sent forth the dove out of the ark;

11   And the dove came in to him in the evening; and, lo, in her mouth *was* an olive leaf plucked off: so Noah knew that the waters were abated from off the earth.

12   And he stayed yet other seven days; and sent forth the dove; which returned not again unto him any more.

13   And it came to pass in the six hundredth and first year, in the first *month*, the first *day* of the month, the waters were dried up from off the earth: and Noah removed the covering of the ark, and looked, and, behold, the face of the ground was dry.

This is generally the last part you hear before Noah is shown leaving the ark. But Noah did not leave the ark at this point. Why? What was he waiting for? He and his sons removed the covering. This sounds like he removed the roof or top of the ark. Yet, even after doing this what was Noah waiting for when he could see outside better?

Noah was told to get on the ark by God. He wanted to make sure he stayed because God had not said to leave the ark. This is not an easy lesson for most of us. But the truth is that God shut the door of the ark. He had not opened it! So, Noah did not have an open door. It was still closed. Noah was waiting on God's timing. Too often today, we are not willing to wait for what is God's timing. We allow anxiety and stress to press us into what we believe are the right things without waiting for that open door. We rush forward into what we believe is next before it is HIS TIMING! Can you imagine how Noah felt waiting months and months on the ark before that jarring rest of the ark on the Mountain? Even then Noah waited three more months before opening a window. Noah was not a man who studied the seas and winds. Yet he rode them out waiting for God's timing.

Dear Lord Jesus,

I know I am impatient. I know I often want things now. Lord, help me to seek YOUR timing not my own. Help me to recognize what I should be doing as I wait. Please don't let me forget that waiting does not mean that you do not care. You care so much to have picked that perfect time just for me! Lord, use me. Put me places where I can share your love.

In Jesus name, Amen.

DAY #28
GENESIS 8:14-22

14   And in the second month, on the seven and twentieth day of the month, was the earth dried.
15   And God spoke unto Noah, saying,
16   Go forth of the ark, you, and your wife, and your sons, and your sons' wives with you.
17   Bring forth with you every living thing that *is* with you, of all flesh, *both* of fowl, and of cattle, and of every creeping thing that creeps upon the earth; that they may breed abundantly in the earth, and be fruitful, and multiply upon the earth.
18   And Noah went forth, and his sons, and his wife, and his sons' wives with him:
19   Every beast, every creeping thing, and every fowl, *and* whatsoever creeps upon the earth, after their kinds, went forth out of the ark.

20	And Noah built an altar unto the LORD; and took of every clean beast, and of every clean fowl, and offered burnt offerings on the altar.
21	And the LORD smelled a sweet savour; and the LORD said in his heart, I will not again curse the ground any more for man's sake; for the imagination of man's heart *is* evil from his youth; neither will I again smite any more every thing living, as I have done.
22	While the earth remains, seedtime and harvest, and cold and heat, and summer and winter, and day and night shall not cease.

Just as God remembered Noah and his family, Noah remembered God and made an offering to Him. This act of thanksgiving and praise for having saved them got a response from God! It was not said out loud but was communicated in his blessing. That message was "I will not again curse the ground for man's sake."

What does God think when we honor him? Verse 21 speaks of the pleasing smell of sacrifice and how it pleased God that Noah gave back to him. It was not required. This was not an admission of sin, but of thanksgiving and praise as stated earlier. God's response was a blessing which will read to tomorrow. This is the first recorded praise offering. When you give a praise or thanksgiving offering you expect nothing in return. It is the same as giving gifts. You should not give them expecting something in return. But something does happen. You are placed on the mind of the person you gave a gift to. Do you want to be on God's mind? Praise HIM!

Dear Lord Jesus,

You bring us through horrible things. You are there with us walking beside us through all the calamities, the joys, the sorrows, and more. Lord, You are always there for me. You never leave me. Lord, thank you for being there through all the horrible things and never once abandoning me. I may have thought it. But I know better. You were even closer to me when I thought all was lost. God, you deserve all my praise!

In Jesus name, Amen.

DAY #29
GENESIS 9:1-7

1   And God blessed Noah and his sons, and said unto them, Be fruitful, and multiply, and replenish the earth.
2   And the fear of you and the dread of you shall be upon every beast of the earth, and upon every fowl of the air, upon all that moves *upon* the earth, and upon all the fishes of the sea; into your hand are they delivered.
3   Every moving thing that lives shall be meat for you; even as the green herb have I given you all things.
4   But flesh with the life thereof, *which is* the blood thereof, shall you not eat.
5   And surely your blood of your lives will I require; at the hand of every beast will I require it, and at the hand of man; at the hand of every man's brother will I require the life of man.

| 6 | Whoso sheds man's blood, by man shall his blood be shed: for in the image of God made he man. |
| 7 | And you, be you fruitful, and multiply; bring forth abundantly in the earth, and multiply therein. |

God gave this blessing to Noah and his sons after Noah gave thanks with an offering. God opened the door, Noah went out and gave thanks and he and his children received a blessing that remains to this day. This blessing includes two prohibitions. 1) Do not kill. 2) This includes not taking your own life (vs. 5). Even animals are not allowed to harm mankind without reprisal. All life is important!

Our lives are not worthless. They are of great value to God. You and I matter to God. Noah had hope when God told him to build an ark. Noah may have felt forgotten on the ark, but his hope was in the day God opened it. Now that the ark is opened God tells them, there is so much more to life, and that they each matter to HIM!

To be given a blessing after being saved from certain death is another example of God's love for us. God could have simply started a new but he chose to save Noah and his family. Then he gave them a blessing that we are still under today! There is no culture that does not have a history recording a world flood. But how many of those stories of a world flood speak of a God that loves us so much that God speaks to the importance of each and every human life on the earth? Our Lord is truly the God of Love!

Dear Lord Jesus,

I may never comprehend how You can love us so much. I may never even understand all that You do for just me. Lord God, please use me to return this blessing of life by allowing me to share this love You have for us. Help me to strengthen those who know You, and lead those who do not yet know You as the God who loves with Your open arms.

In Jesus name, Amen.

DAY #30
GENESIS 9:8-17

8   And God spoke unto Noah, and to his sons with him, saying,
9   And I, behold, I establish my covenant with you, and with your seed after you;
10 And with every living creature that *is* with you, of the fowl, of the cattle, and of every beast of the earth with you; from all that go out of the ark, to every beast of the earth.
11 And I will establish my covenant with you; neither shall all flesh be cut off any more by the waters of a flood; neither shall there any more be a flood to destroy the earth.
12 And God said, This *is* the token of the covenant which I make between me and you and every living creature that *is* with you, for perpetual generations:
13 I do set my bow in the cloud, and it shall be for a token of a covenant between me and the earth.
14 And it shall come to pass, when I bring a cloud over the earth, that the bow shall be seen in the cloud:
15 And I will remember my covenant, which *is* between me and you and every living creature of all flesh; and the waters shall no more become a flood to destroy all flesh.

16   And the bow shall be in the cloud; and I will look upon it, that I may remember the ever-lasting covenant between God and every living creature of all flesh that *is* upon the earth.

17   And God said unto Noah, This *is* the token of the covenant, which I have established between me and all flesh that *is* upon the earth.

To think that today, a community whose very premise for its existence denies the ability of God to bless us as HE wishes, to "be fruitful, and multiply, and replenish the earth," adopted the symbol of God's promise (the rainbow) to Noah and his sons, which includes us is a sad reflection on the state of man today. Is the world replenished today? We no longer live hundreds of years. In many countries today both parents produce only one or two children. There are a few exceptions.

God's covenant was a promise to all living creatures that He would never send a world flood to destroy all flesh again. Think about this. Every time rain falls today we do not always see a rainbow at the end. But, it is possible even today! There is science to explain the appearance of the rainbow, how it can be seen, and why the colors appear in a certain order every time. These scientific "revelations" explain the why. But they miss one important thing. That God is a God of love. His promises can be trusted. God is a God of order, because of this they can use the scientific method to discover things. If things were in a constant state of flux, they could not have a science, because the laws of science would be constantly changing. Even the human concept of random has order.

Dear Lord Jesus,

You know us more than we know ourselves. Lord, help me to stand and never forget what You have done for me. You set an example of what it means "to keep your word." Lord, may my words be true, and may my work be trusted.

In Jesus name, Amen.

DAY #31
GENESIS 9:18-29

18   And the sons of Noah, that went forth of the ark, were Shem, and Ham, and Japheth: and Ham *is* the father of Canaan.
19   These *are* the three sons of Noah: and of them was the whole earth overspread.
20   And Noah began *to be* an husbandman, and he planted a vineyard:
21   And he drank of the wine, and was drunken; and he was uncovered within his tent.
22   And Ham, the father of Canaan, saw the nakedness of his father, and told his two brethren without.
23   And Shem and Japheth took a garment, and laid *it* upon both their shoulders, and went backward, and covered the nakedness of their father; and their faces *were* backward, and they saw not their father's nakedness.
24   And Noah awoke from his wine, and knew what his younger son had done unto him.
25   And he said, Cursed *be* Canaan; a servant of servants shall he be unto his brethren.

26 And he said, Blessed *be* the LORD God of Shem; and Canaan shall be his servant.
27 God shall enlarge Japheth, and he shall dwell in the tents of Shem; and Canaan shall be his servant.
28 And Noah lived after the flood three hundred and fifty years.
29 And all the days of Noah were nine hundred and fifty years: and he died.

What happened here is that Noah got drunk. Some claim there was no drunkenness before this time, simply because it is not recorded in the Bible. We can't know the answer if that is true or not. It is not worth our time to debate. Regardless, Noah got drunk and drunkenness is a sin. Noah was not perfect. Only God is perfect. As a result of his sin, Noah curses not Ham, but Ham's son Canaan. Some people miss this and claim that is the reason black people were slaves. No, Ham was not cursed, only his son Canaan was cursed. J. Vernon McGee points out that the Israelites left Egypt and came to … "the Land of Canaan." When Israel was established some people remained as servants, due to the sins of Israel and those of the Canaanites.

Japheth is also skipped over, as stated earlier Japheth was the oldest, but does not get the special blessing due to being the oldest. Shem, the middle child, receives that special blessing. Shem stood out to Noah as special.

Dear Lord Jesus,

Help me to become one that seeks not only knowledge of Your Word but to place Your Word in my heart. Lord, Your Word should resonate throughout my being so that I am compelled to share it, that others may learn of Your great love.

In Jesus name, Amen.

DAY #32
GENESIS 10:1-32

1   Now these *are* the generations of the sons of Noah, Shem, Ham, and Japheth: and unto them were sons born after the flood.
2   The sons of Japheth; Gomer, and Magog, and Madai, and Javan, and Tubal, and Meshech, and Tiras.
3   And the sons of Gomer; Ashkenaz, and Riphas, and Togarmah.
4   And the sons of Javan; Elishah, and Tarshish, Kittim, and Dodanim.
5   By these were the isles of the Gentiles divided in their lands; every one after his tongue, after their families, in their nations.
6   And the sons of Ham; Cush, and Mizraim, and Phut, and Canaan.
7   And the sons of Cush; Seba, and Havilah, and Sabtah, and Raamah, and Sabtecha: and the sons of Raamah; Sheba, and Dedan.
8   And Cush begat Nimrod: he began to be a mighty one in the earth.
9   He was a mighty hunter before the LORD: why it is said, Even as Nimrod the mighty hunter before the LORD.

10   And the beginning of his kingdom was Babel, and Erech, and Accad, and Calneh, in the land of Shinar.

11   Out of that land went forth Asshur, and built Nineveh, and the city Rehoboth, and Calah,

12   And Resen between Nineveh and Calah: the same *is* a great city.

13   And Mizraim begat Ludim, and Anamim, and Lehabim, and Naphtuhim,

14   And Pathrusim, and Casluhim, (out of whom came Philistim,) and Caphtorim.

15   And Canaan begat Sidon his firstborn, and Heth,

16   And the Jebusite, and the Amorite, and the Girgasite,

17   And the Hivite, and the Arkite, and the Sinite,

18   And the Arvadite, and the Zemarite, and the Hamathite: and afterward were the families of the Canaanites spread abroad.

19   And the border of the Canaanites was from Sidon, as you comest to Gerar, unto Gaza; as you goes, unto Sodom, and Gomorrah, and Admah, and Zeboim, even unto Lasha.

20   These *are* the sons of Ham, after their families, after their tongues, in their countries, *and* in their nations.

21   Unto Shem also, the father of all the children of Eber, the brother of Japheth the elder, even to him were *children* born.

22   The children of Shem; Elam, and Asshur, and Arphaxad, and Lud, and Aram.

23   And the children of Aram; Uz, and Hul, and Gether, and Mash.

24   And Arphaxad begat Salah; and Salah begat Eber.

25   And unto Eber were born two sons: the name of one *was* Peleg; for in his days was the earth divided; and his brother's name *was* Joktan.

26   And Joktan begat Almodad, and Sheleph, and Hazarmaveth, and Jerah,

27	And Hadoram, and Uzal, and Diklah,
28	And Obal, and Abimael, and Sheba,
29	And Ophir, and Havilah, and Jobab: all these *were* the sons of Joktan.
30	And their dwelling was from Mesha, as you goes unto Sephar a mount of the east.
31	These *are* the sons of Shem, after their families, after their tongues, in their lands, after their nations.
32	These *are* the families of the sons of Noah, after their generations, in their nations: and by these were the nations divided in the earth after the flood.

One of the interesting points about this chapter is that it speaks of different languages before the concept is introduced. My thoughts on why this was done, was to answer a child's question "where do we come from?" The names given and the locations given speak of large areas of the world still in existence today. Shem's family settled in an area known as Mesopotamia, in Social Studies classes this area was called the "Fertile Crescent." Ham's family settled in the land of Canaan which Israel later is given as the Promised Land and South. Japheth's descendants are stated to end up north some in Russia

In verse 25, is the time period given for our concept today of one continent (Pangea) dividing up and becoming seven continents. Today this is taught as continental plate drift theory in science classes. But it is actually Biblically accurate.

I recommend reading https://askjohnmackay.com/if-all-races-originated-from-noahs-sons-why-are-there-such-big-differences-between-the-races for further study.

Dear Lord Jesus,

You answer our questions in the best manner. Sometimes we simply need to hear your answer and then think about the order in which you answered our questions. You even teach us special lessons through that! Lord God, You love us so much, You even put golden nuggets to be found in the study of Your Word. Lord, thank you for planting so many special things in Your Word, that it truly remains new to us every time we read it! Lord, help me to share the wonders of Your Word that I learn today.

In Jesus name, Amen.

DAY #33
GENESIS 11:1-9

1 And the whole earth was of one language, and of one speech.
2 And it came to pass, as they journeyed from the east, that they found a plain in the land of Shinar; and they dwelt there.
3 And they said one to another, Go to, let us make brick, and burn them thoroughly. And they had brick for stone, and slime had they for mortar.
4 And they said, Go to, let us build us a city and a tower, whose top *may reach* unto heaven; and let us make us a name, lest we be scattered abroad upon the face of the whole earth.
5 And the LORD came down to see the city and the tower, which the children of men built.

6	And the LORD said, Behold, the people *is* one, and they have all one language; and this they begin to do: and now nothing will be restrained from them, which they have imagined to do.
7	Go to, let us go down, and there confound their language, that they may not understand one another's speech.
8	So the LORD scattered them abroad from there upon the face of all the earth: and they left off to build the city.
9	Therefore is the name of it called Babel; because the LORD did there confound the language of all the earth: and from there did the LORD scatter them abroad upon the face of all the earth.

The Tower of Babel, or should we say the tower of foolish ambition. When we seek to honor ourselves, we construct a "Tower of Babel." Look at the self-fulfilled prophecy claimed in verse 4 not God, but by the foolish men: "*let us build us a city and a tower, whose top may reach unto heaven; and let us make us a name, lest we be scattered abroad upon the face of the whole earth.*"

The Lord God loved us so much that this incident is not recalled with fear. The non-stop building was left for an inability to communicate. People did not even think about how to communicate with those who could not understand them. It created a sense of fear, driving men to seek out their wives and children, and finding comfort when they too could comprehend each other! God instituted the family. He would not tear that apart! Families and groups of families were kept together. If anything, this event of foolish ambition resulted in God pulling the people from serving foolish ambition back to taking care of themselves and their families.

The dispersal of the families into clans and groups says something about how the lack of communication was also seen as possibly miscommunicating words and thoughts into things that offended each other. Being offended is not a reason to run off. It is a reason to try to communicate better and clearer. If you have an idea that improves life, like the usage of coal to heat a home should you run away if the person misunderstands you and seems offended while living in the cold, or should you try again so you can help bring them out of the cold? If people are offended because you share Christ, does that mean you should shut up, or does that mean you should change strategies to try to reach them?

Dear Lord Jesus,

You are the God of LOVE! Even through our own foolish ambitions, You stay by our sides working to bring us home. Help us Lord, set our priorities straight. Help us to put You first and our families next. Keep us from the foolish ambitions and distractions that lead us away from You and our loved ones.

In Jesus name, Amen.

DAY #34
GENESIS 11:10-28

10   These *are* the generations of Shem: Shem *was* an hundred years old, and begat Arphaxad two years after the flood:
11   And Shem lived after he begat Arphaxad five hundred years, and begat sons and daughters.
12   And Arphaxad lived five and thirty years, and begat Salah:

13   And Arphaxad lived after he begat Salah four hundred and three years, and begat sons and daughters.
14   And Salah lived thirty years, and begat Eber:
15   And Salah lived after he begat Eber four hundred and three years, and begat sons and daughters.
16   And Eber lived four and thirty years, and begat Peleg:
17   And Eber lived after he begat Peleg four hundred and thirty years, and begat sons and daughters.
18   And Peleg lived thirty years, and begat Reu:
19   And Peleg lived after he begat Reu two hundred and nine years, and begat sons and daughters.
20   And Reu lived two and thirty years, and begat Serug:
21   And Reu lived after he begat Serug two hundred and seven years, and begat sons and daughters.
22   And Serug lived thirty years, and begat Nahor:
23   And Serug lived after he begat Nahor two hundred years, and begat sons and daughters.
24   And Nahor lived nine and twenty years, and begat Terah:
25   And Nahor lived after he begat Terah an hundred and nineteen years, and begat sons and daughters.
26   And Terah lived seventy years, and begat Abram, Nahor, and Haran.
27   Now these *are* the generations of Terah: Terah begat Abram, Nahor, and Haran; and Haran begat Lot.
28   And Haran died before his father Terah in the land of his nativity, in Ur of the Chaldees.
29   And Abram and Nahor took them wives: the name of Abram's wife *was* Sarai; and the name of Nahor's wife, Milcah, the daughter of Haran, the father of Milcah, and the father of Iscah.
30   But Sarai was barren; she *had* no child.
31   And Terah took Abram his son, and Lot the son of Haran his son's son, and Sarai his daughter in law, his son

Abram's wife; and they went forth with them from Ur of the Chaldees, to go into the land of Canaan; and they came unto Haran, and dwelt there.

32   And the days of Terah were two hundred and five years: and Terah died in Haran.

Almost 300 years have passed since the flood before Abram was born. 292 years passed. It appears, that Abram is one of a set of triplets. Since Terah's sons were all born when he turned seventy. This passage explains some of what is to come in the following chapters. Abram's brother Haran, dies before Terah and Abram leaves Ur. This is important because it explains the closeness of Lot to Abram. He is the uncle. Lot is the son of his dead brother, Haran. Twins and triplets are very close. They have a special bond after growing up together. Haran's death leaves a hole in Abram's heart.

When Terah and Abram (and his wife Sarai) leave Ur, they also leave behind Nahor who married a woman whose father had the same first name as his dead brother. Terah was leaving behind two sons, but his son Abram and grandson Lot would come with them, filling that void.

Dear Lord Jesus,

This history is so exact. We can know exactly what year the flood happened. We can know exactly when Abraham walked the earth. We can even go farther back thanks to the incredible details left in your book. You even go so far as to give us histories that reveal the sadness of loss, that explain what can be confusing later on. Your Word is a marvel of wonders! So much is there to be found! Lord, help me to share these wonders found in Your Word.

In Jesus name, Amen.

DAY #35
GENESIS 12:1-5

1   Now the LORD had said unto Abram, Get you out of your country, and from your kindred, and from your father's house, unto a land that I will show you:
2   And I will make of you a great nation, and I will bless you, and make your name great; and you shall be a blessing:
3   And I will bless them that bless you, and curse him that curses you: and in you shall all families of the earth be blessed.
4   So Abram departed, as the LORD had spoken unto him; and Lot went with him: and Abram *was* seventy and five years old when he departed out of Haran.
5   And Abram took Sarai his wife, and Lot his brother's son, and all their substance that they had gathered, and the souls that they had gotten in Haran; and they went forth to go into the land of Canaan; and into the land of Canaan they came.

When God speaks to Abram he says, "*Get you out of your country, and from your kindred, and from your father's house.*" Abram does not willingly follow all of what God has asked. Lot is part of the kindred he has been asked to leave behind. Too many times our stubbornness gets in the way of God blessing us. We don't want to do exactly what God wants. This is a good example of this. Abram was told, leave your kindred. That means his relations. Lot was not his own son, though he treated him as the child he and Sarai did not have. Partially following God's requests delays blessings. Sometimes we need to sit and think about the things we have done and how, if we had just done what God asked of us, instead of … what might have happened. We do know that in verse 2, God promised to make Abram a great nation. But he had no son. In fact, the promise of a son does not come to reality until Abram is 100 years old! So, why not reflect back? What if Abram had left Lot behind? The truth is that if he had done that, he would not have grown into the man he became. God did not correct him, but let him see a reason for separation in time. God works on each of us in HIS time, not ours. He knows what will take time for us to learn and grasp, and what we will know and understand quickly.

Dear Lord Jesus,

You know where we are. You see us in our worst moments and in our best. Yet, You are always there for us. You even stand by us in our stubbornness trying to show us a way out of our foolishness when we plug our ears and try to continue in our own way. Lord, THANK YOU for not giving up on us! Your love is special! It beats down our anger. It melts hatred with hugs that can only be felt by Your embrace. Lord, please keep working on me.

In Jesus name, Amen.

DAY #36
GENESIS 12:6-10

6 And Abram passed through the land unto the place of Sichem, unto the plain of Moreh. And the Canaanite *was* then in the land.
7 And the LORD appeared unto Abram, and said, Unto your seed will I give this land: and there built he an altar unto the LORD, who appeared unto him.
8 And he removed from there unto a mountain on the east of Bethel, and pitched his tent, *having*] Bethel on the west, and Hai on the east: and there he built an altar unto the LORD, and called upon the name of the LORD.
9 And Abram journeyed, going on still toward the south.
10 And there was a famine in the land: and Abram went down into Egypt to sojourn there; for the famine *was* grievous in the land.

Abram has traveled from Mesopotamia to Canaan. This is not a small journey. It is here that God tells Abram *"unto your seed will I give this land."* Sometimes, we not only need to pay attention to what is said but what is missing. Missing is that Abram was not given the land. His seed, in the future, would be given the land. When you first read verses 6-8, you think Abram is about to set up camp and reside there for the rest of his days. Verse 9 then comes as a surprise. Why is he moving South??? Abram listened well to God this time. Abram who is over 100 years old now, says that, he himself was not given the land which his seed will inherit. So, he moves on. Mankind are creatures of habit. We have established routines and they help us get through the day. Abram had so constantly been on the move, it may have been more comfortable to push on. Keep in mind that we are not just talking about Abram, Sarai, and Lot. We are talking about a few hundred people who were part of their group. A routine established makes people comfortable. They can expect what is coming.

Abram's journey into Canaan allowed him to see the land his children would be given. It also put him in a situation where he was responsible for not just himself and his own family, but for the entire group that was in a land suffering from famine. He may have wanted to stay and see that land, but famine was there. Sometimes God does things to make us move on. We get comfortable someplace and want to stay, but the situation changes so much that God pushes us on, in the right direction.

Dear Lord Jesus,

You are with me throughout my entire day even when I am asleep You are there. Your Word says it is not in man to direct his own steps (Jer. 10:23). Lord, direct my steps. Lead me from foolishness. Lead me on the straightway that gives You the glory! Lord, in doing this help me to point others to seek Your face also.

In Jesus name, Amen.

DAY #37
GENESIS 12:11-20

11 And it came to pass, when he was come near to enter into Egypt, that he said unto Sarai his wife, Behold now, I know that you *are* a fair woman to look upon:
12 Therefore it shall come to pass, when the Egyptians shall see you, that they shall say, This *is* his wife: and they will kill me, but they will save you alive.
13 Say, I pray you, you *are* my sister: that it may be well with me for your sake; and my soul shall live because of you.
14 And it came to pass, that, when Abram was come into Egypt, the Egyptians beheld the woman that she *was* very fair.
15 The princes also of Pharaoh saw her, and commended her before Pharaoh: and the woman was taken into Pharaoh's house.
16 And he entreated Abram well for her sake: and he had sheep, and oxen, and he asses, and menservants, and maidservants, and she asses, and camels.
17 And the LORD plagued Pharaoh and his house with great plagues because of Sarai Abram's wife.
18 And Pharaoh called Abram, and said, What *is* this *that* you have done unto me? why did you not tell me that she *was* your wife?
19 Why did you say, She *is* my sister? so I might have taken her to me to wife: now therefore behold your wife, take *her*, and go your way.
20 And Pharaoh commanded *his* men concerning him: and they sent him away, and his wife, and all that he had.

When you think about the background to this story you start to marvel at God's miracles. Sarai was no spring chicken, neither was Abram who was over seventy-five years old! Yet there was no mistake that Sarai was seen as an amazing woman of beauty. But not only was she seen as a beauty Abram was seen of like age and was able to be called brother. This seems like a miracle in itself, but Abram and Sarai did not see themselves as old either. The aging process must have been a lot different back then.

Abram gets a lot of criticism here for not trusting God to be his protector. He recognized his wife was a gorgeous beauty, and knew the pharaoh would send his men to claim her even if this meant killing him, so he played the part of being her brother. It isn't long before Abram is proven correct and they come and take Sarai.

Abram is sent gifts, and "maintained" by Egypt's royalty as a result. Remember the reason stated for coming to Egypt, was a famine in Canaan. Yet, through this horror of having Sarai ripped away from him. Abram must have kept his wife in his prayers before God. God was not absent. It was not like God did not see what Abram planned or what had happened. It is not like God did not keep Sarai safe. Miraculously, Sarai is preserved and kept safe. Only God's hand of protection could do that. God saw all this and sent GREAT plagues upon Egypt until Sarai was returned.

All through this visit to Egypt they are both blessed and provided for during the time of trial. Now they are rejected and sent out of Egypt. This testing … or time of trial proved that God stood in the gap for them. God intervened. When Abram was powerless, it was God who acted!

Dear Lord Jesus,

Sometimes I make bad choices and do not trust you to take care of things. Yet, You stand be me, watching over me, and still push me back to the realization I should have trusted You in the first place. Lord, I want to get things right. I want to stop getting things wrong the first time. Lord, help me to see Your will and desires. Mold me to seek You in ways I had not thought of before.

In Jesus name, Amen.

DAY #38
GENESIS 13:1-5

1   And Abram went up out of Egypt, he, and his wife, and all that he had, and Lot with him, into the south.
2   And Abram *was* very rich in cattle, in silver, and in gold.
3   And he went on his journeys from the south even to Bethel, unto the place where his tent had been at the beginning, between Bethel and Hai;
4   Unto the place of the altar, which he had made there at the first: and there Abram called on the name of the LORD.
5   And Lot also, which went with Abram, had flocks, and herds, and tents.

This is interesting in that Abram leaves Egypt and does not build an altar and give thanks to God after leaving Egypt. Instead, he returned to where God had talked to him and to the altar he built before the famine came and compelled him into Egypt. This passage sounds like there was a sense of immediacy to return to that place. Abram may have been running to the comfort he remembered as he felt the presence of God, after having almost lost everything, that everything being his life and his wife.

In this short passage, Lot is noted as being with Abram not once but twice. Remember Abram was supposed to have left him behind some time ago. There is also an emphasis here on Abram's wealth, which is symbolic of God having blessed him. Lot too has wealth, which is noted here differently. Note what is missing: silver and gold. This gives a clue about what is to come. This little hint implies that it is possible Lot does not manage money well.

Dear Lord Jesus,

You are my strong fortress. You are my place of comfort, my tower of refuge. Lord, please help me to put you first in all things. Lord, I know that You lead my footsteps into that which is good and right for me. Lord help me to only follow the path You set out for me. Keep me from my own foolishness, that distracts me from that which You desire for me.

In Jesus name, Amen.

DAY #39
GENESIS 13:6-13

6 And the land was not able to bear them, that they might dwell together: for their substance was great, so that they could not dwell together.
7 And there was a strife between the herdsmen of Abram's cattle and the herdsmen of Lot's cattle: and the Canaanite and the Perizzite dwelled then in the land.

8   And Abram said unto Lot, Let there be no strife, I pray you, between me and you, and between my herdsmen and your herdsmen; for we *be* brethren.
9   Is not the whole land before you? separate yourself, I pray you, from me: if *you will take* the left hand, then I will go to the right; or if *you depart* to the right hand, then I will go to the left.
10 And Lot lifted up his eyes, and beheld all the plain of Jordan, that it *was* well watered every where, before the LORD destroyed Sodom and Gomorrah, *even* as the garden of the LORD, like the land of Egypt, as you come unto Zoar.
11 Then Lot chose him all the plain of Jordan; and Lot journeyed east: and they separated themselves the one from the other.
12 Abram dwelled in the land of Canaan, and Lot dwelled in the cities of the plain, and pitched *his* tent toward Sodom.
13 But the men of Sodom *were* wicked and sinners before the LORD exceedingly.

Sometimes when we do not make a choice we need to, God puts us in a place we have no option but to make the choice he wants. Abram was supposed to leave Lot back when he started his journey. But no. He chose not to fully obey God. When God told him about the blessing of the land for his children, Abram was not receiving that land! Could it be because Abram was in rebellion still having Lot with him? When they returned to that place where God spoke to Abram after leaving Egypt, God put Abram in that place to do what HE wanted. God is patient. Our timing is not the best. But God is willing to work on us and help us get where he wants us to be.

Dear Lord Jesus,

Thank you for loving me so much. I have done nothing to deserve such love. You even take the time to mold me from within. You make the inside better so the rest of me shines. Lord, please keep working on me. Help me to be the one who plants the seeds of Your love thanks to Your work on me.

In Jesus name, Amen.

DAY #40
GENESIS 13:14-18

14   And the LORD said unto Abram, after that Lot was separated from him, Lift up now yours eyes, and look from the place where you are northward, and southward, and eastward, and westward:
15   For all the land which you see, to you will I give it, and to your seed forever.
16   And I will make your seed as the dust of the earth: so that if a man can number the dust of the earth, *then* shall your seed also be numbered.
17   Arise, walk through the land in the length of it and in the breadth of it; for I will give it unto you.
18   Then Abram removed *his* tent, and came and dwelt in the plain of Mamre, which *is* in Hebron, and built there an altar unto the LORD.

Sometimes God waits on us to do the one thing he asked. He may constantly be reminding us that we need to do that one thing, but that is only because we refuse to listen. Abram refused to listen for some time. How long the Bible does not tell us, but this seems to be in years not months. God waits – then we finally do as he asked…HE BLESSES US! In truth, this should make us feel stupid for not getting the message earlier. We should feel repentant for our stubborn refusal to obey. God could put it all in our face and say, "I told you so! Do you remember how long ago I told you this?" This is a God that allows us to make stupid and bad choices for ourselves. Why? Because the one and only true God loves us enough to let us learn from our mistakes. Hopefully, we learn and do not repeat those mistakes.

This time around, the blessing God gives Abram of this land, is not only to his children, it is to him also. God could not give this promise to Abram before, because he treated Lot like his own son, whom he did not have. Lot, This speaks to God's holiness, His pureness, and that He desires for us to be like-minded with Him.

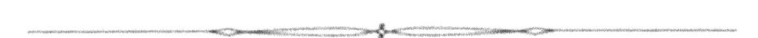

Dear Lord Jesus,

Help me to listen to You better. I am not asking for You to open my open my ears. I am asking You to push me into obeying Your wisdom and guidance more so now than ever. Lord, remove my stubborn refusals, my foolish desires that are not yours. Lead my steps in the way You want me to go.

In Jesus name, Amen.

DAY #41
GENESIS 14:1-7

1 And it came to pass in the days of Amraphel king of Shinar, Arioch king of Ellasar, Chedorlaomer king of Elam, and Tidal king of nations;
2 *That these* made war with Bera king of Sodom, and with Birsha king of Gomorrah, Shinab king of Admah, and Shemeber king of Zeboiim, and the king of Bela, which is Zoar.
3 All these were joined together in the vale of Siddim, which is the salt sea.
4 Twelve years they served Chedorlaomer, and in the thirteenth year they rebelled.
5 And in the fourteenth year came Chedorlaomer, and the kings that *were* with him, and smote the Rephaims in Ashteroth Karnaim, and the Zuzims in Ham, and the Emims in Shaveh Kiriathaim,
6 And the Horites in their mount Seir, unto Elparan, which *is* by the wilderness.
7 And they returned, and came to Enmishpat, which *is* Kadesh, and smote all the country of the Amalekites, and also the Amorites, that dwelt in Hazezontamar.

When the Bible gives you background history to a story, there is a guarantee that there is a gold nugget hidden in it. Here are just a few:

1) The very first name mentioned here is Amraphel king of Shinar, according to some noted scholars, this is Hammurabi, King of Babylon (https://www.jewishencyclopedia.com/articles/1440-amraphel). Hammurabi the "lawgiver," who everyone learns about in High School. He is credited with having written the first set of laws now known as Hammurabi's Code. Hammurabi is thought to have ruled Babylon around 2376-2333 B.C.
2) Arioch, King of Ellasar is believed to be Eri-aku, king of Larsa. Eri-aku,s kingdom was later conquered by Hammurabi.
3) Chedorlaomer king of Elam, little is known of him, but it is thought that Elam was in Persia, now known as Iran.
4) Tidal king of *Goyim* nations is thought to have been Tudhaliya, a proto-Hittite King. There were a few sharing the shortened version of the name Tudal.

These details verify the events that took place. We can verify that the people existed. A classical text from Jewish literature actually plays with the name Bera and says it means Evil Son (https://shorturl.at/hS015). The mention of Admah and Zeboiim is also significant historically, as these cities were destroyed along with Sodom and Gomorrah.

Don't just read through the scriptures. Dig into them. Learn more.

Dear Lord Jesus,

Thank you for teaching me how important details can be. You show us how real Your Word is and how it can be proven accurate historically. Lord, You do so much to show us You are real and that

You love us use me, Lord, that I may be one to share this incredible love You have.

In Jesus name, Amen.

DAY #42
GENESIS 14:8-17

8   And there went out the king of Sodom, and the king of Gomorrah, and the king of Admah, and the king of Zeboiim, and the king of Bela (the same *is* Zoar;) and they joined battle with them in the vale of Siddim;
9   With Chedorlaomer the king of Elam, and with Tidal king of nations, and Amraphel king of Shinar, and Arioch king of Ellasar; four kings with five.
10 And the vale of Siddim *was full of* slimepits; and the kings of Sodom and Gomorrah fled, and fell there; and they that remained fled to the mountain.
11 And they took all the goods of Sodom and Gomorrah, and all their victuals, and went their way.
12 And they took Lot, Abram's brother's son, who dwelt in Sodom, and his goods, and departed.
13 And there came one that had escaped, and told Abram the Hebrew; for he dwelt in the plain of Mamre the Amorite, brother of Eshcol, and brother of Aner: and these *were* confederate with Abram.
14 And when Abram heard that his brother was taken captive, he armed his trained *servants*, born in his own house, three hundred and eighteen, and pursued *them* unto Dan.

15 And he divided himself against them, he and his servants, by night, and smote them, and pursued them unto Hobah, which *is* on the left hand of Damascus.
16 And he brought back all the goods, and also brought again his brother Lot, and his goods, and the women also, and the people.
17 And the king of Sodom went out to meet him after his return from the slaughter of Chedorlaomer, and of the kings that *were* with him, at the valley of Shaveh, which *is* the king's dale.

Remember that these Kings are not unknown today. Hammurabi was Amraphel. It is important to think of this not just as scripture, but as a historical event that should be taught in schools because it ties much of history together that is taught today.

Lot chose to go to Sodom. He chose to place himself amidst a city of people known for their perversions. They are not remembered for their strength or security. Sodom and Gomorrah were sacked, the two cities were plundered, all the goods, and many of the people were taken. This was part of the conquest ethic that ruled. It was why kings bound together to battle against others. It was recognition that by themselves they were not able to fight against a strong enemy. If Lot considered being with Abram, his uncle, being a place of safety, then maybe he thought being in a city where multiple kings bound together to protect each other was a place of safety. But was it?

Scripture records Abram's hearing of Lot being taken a bit differently than we would expect. Verse 14 says: "And when Abram heard that his brother was taken captive." It does not say "Abram heard that his nephew…." It says, brother. Cain asked, "Am I my brother's keeper?" Abram does not even think to ask that question. He acts! YES, HE IS HIS BROTHER'S KEEPER!

Today, many Christian men allow themselves to feel alone in their struggles. Abram's vicious fight FOR HIS BROTHER is the reason Christian men should not stand idly by when a brother is struggling with things like addiction. We CAN help! We can go out and fight for them too! Ladies, please understand this is something men do more than women because we are not as social as you are. We keep a lot of things just to ourselves. We need our brothers to be our keepers whether we know it or not. We need men like Abram to get in the fight to save us from our stupid stubbornness as we go do the wrong path.

Are you on the wrong path? Find a good brother in Christ to help you get stronger!

If you are on the right path following Christ, who are you helping and who is your brother that is helping you grow and sharpen in the faith?

Dear Lord Jesus,

Thank you for putting Abram in the right place and having him teach us we should not question if we are our brother's keeper. Thank you for this important recording of history where kings were beaten by one man's determination to save his brother. Lord, use us so that we can share YOUR love which is so much more than anything we ourselves can offer the world.

In Jesus name, Amen.

DAY #43
GENESIS 14:18-24

18   And Melchizedek king of Salem brought forth bread and wine: and he *was* the priest of the most high God.
19   And he blessed him, and said, Blessed *be* Abram of the most high God, possessor of heaven and earth:
20   And blessed be the most high God, which has delivered yours enemies into your hand. And he gave him tithes of all.
21   And the king of Sodom said unto Abram, Give me the persons, and take the goods to yourself.
22   And Abram said to the king of Sodom, I have lift up mine hand unto the LORD, the most high God, the possessor of heaven and earth,
23   That I will not *take* from a thread even to a shoelatchet, and that I will not take any thing that *is* yours, lest you should say, I have made Abram rich:
24   Save only that which the young men have eaten, and the portion of the men which went with me, Aner, Eshcol, and Mamre; let them take their portion.

Abram has returned from the battle as his brother's keeper (of Lot). This was not a battle to attain wealth. Abram has returned. People knew where he lived and where he would return. This explains the vicious part of the battle when Abram chose to battle as his brother's keeper he knew it involved risk. This battle meant he had to go into this planning to take out an enemy that could strike back should they be able to gather forces and name their attackers.

Abram is now met by Melchizedek, King of Salm, priest of the most high God, the God who promised Abram and his children the land. This was before Moses, this was before the law was given, and yet Abram gave a tenth of his income to Melchizedek. This is the beginning of tithing. God blessed Abram with a great amount. When you think of how this passage seems to flow easily, You start to wonder if that 10 percent was set at the beginning of the caravan back. Abram had planned to give the 10 percent back to God. He never considered it to be his.

The other kings watching this unfold must have been surprised. Next up was the king of Sodom. Abram saw this man as evil, and would not take payment from an evil man the implication would be that he worked for an evil unrepentant man. The king of Sodom could have claimed he paid Abram to save everyone. Abram had given glory to God by giving a tenth! Would it not be the same as spitting on God, to accept this evil man's gifts?

Dear Lord Jesus,

You changed the game with Abram. You raised up a man who understood that we must stand in the gap for our brethren. We are our brother's keepers. We cannot abandon those close to us. Lord, help me to strengthen others. Use me that I may be a man who puts helping others grow in YOU as one of my largest priorities.

In Jesus name, Amen.

DAY #44
GENESIS 15:1-6

1   After these things the word of the LORD came unto Abram in a vision, saying, Fear not, Abram: I *am* your shield, *and* your exceeding great reward.
2   And Abram said, Lord GOD, what will you give me, seeing I go childless, and the steward of my house *is* this Eliezer of Damascus?
3   And Abram said, Behold, to me you have given no seed: and, lo, one born in my house is mine heir.
4   And, behold, the word of the LORD *came* unto him, saying, This shall not be yours heir; but he that shall come forth out of yours own bowels shall be yours heir.
5   And he brought him forth abroad, and said, Look now toward heaven, and tell the stars, if you be able to number them: and he said unto him, So shall your seed be.
6   And he believed in the LORD; and he counted it to him for righteousness.

Here we have part one of a conversation between Abram and God. Abram is told, "I am your great reward." Abram can only think in terms of this present world. It is as if he has no concept of an afterlife. For he takes the reward God promises him and thinks, "what good is a reward? I am an old man with no children to inherit this reward." We humans often want things now, not in HIS timing but in our timing, and that means now. Abram was over 100. Sarai is not a young woman also. God responds giving Abram assurance that he will have an heir. What is interesting is that both Abram and God speak of only one heir. One child to pass this promise, this reward down to, so that the prophecies may come to pass. This singular complaint, or request as it may be requires a miracle. It requires God to act. Yet, Abram believes after God shows him the stars. Abram did not require more. He just believed. The Lord, "counted it to him for righteousness."

Dear Lord Jesus,

Help me to see Your desires for me as real, so much so that I feel that I can touch what You desire for me to do. Lord, help my unbelief. Help me to run forward and embrace that which you have set for me to do. I want to be better than I am. Mold me and make me after YOUR will. Help me to see that Your ways are better. Help me to take steps forward sharing your love, and helping others to grow deeper in Your love.

In Jesus name, Amen.

DAY #45
GENESIS 15:7-21

7   And he said unto him, I *am* the LORD that brought you out of Ur of the Chaldees, to give you this land to inherit it.

8   And he said, Lord GOD, whereby shall I know that I shall inherit it?

9   And he said unto him, Take me an heifer of three years old, and a she goat of three years old, and a ram of three years old, and a turtledove, and a young pigeon.
10   And he took unto him all these, and divided them in the midst, and laid each piece one against another: but the birds divided he not.
11   And when the fowls came down upon the carcases, Abram drove them away.
12   And when the sun was going down, a deep sleep fell upon Abram; and, lo, an horror of great darkness fell upon him.
13   And he said unto Abram, Know of a surety that your seed shall be a stranger in a land *that is* not theirs, and shall serve them; and they shall afflict them four hundred years;
14   And also that nation, whom they shall serve, will I judge: and afterward shall they come out with great substance.
15   And you shall go to your fathers in peace; you shall be buried in a good old age.
16   But in the fourth generation they shall come here again: for the iniquity of the Amorites *is* not yet full.
17   And it came to pass, that, when the sun went down, and it was dark, behold a smoking furnace, and a burning lamp that passed between those pieces.
18   In the same day the LORD made a covenant with Abram, saying, Unto your seed have I given this land, from the river of Egypt unto the great river, the river Euphrates:
19   The Kenites, and the Kenizzites, and the Kadmonites,
20   And the Hittites, and the Perizzites, and the Rephaims,
21   And the Amorites, and the Canaanites, and the Girgashites, and the Jebusites.

Belief is in that which we cannot see, or touch. It may be in some future event, or in God himself, but that faith does not require evidence. Yet, God made us in such a way, that we mere humans like evidence. Abram's faith was firm that God had said this to him. God even recognized that faith. But Abram asked for a sign. This sign may have been something he could show his wife, Sarai, or something to strengthen him when his faith was weaker. God never questioned this. He agrees to it!

Abram then gets directions to prepare a sacrifice. He follows every direction. Then like an expectant father in a waiting room, sat watching, pacing, waiting for that sign. It took longer than he wanted, it took at least long enough that birds dared to come down onto the prepared sacrifice. Abram quickly scared them off. This is another example of God teaching that his timing is better than our timing. Abram may have rushed at getting that sacrifice ready, but made sure it was done to the best of his ability. After all, God said yes to his request for a sign. He sat there expecting a sign, God promised one. He dashed away those things that would dare pick at what he offered God.

"An horror of great darkness fell upon him." This was within Abram's sleep. If you have never experienced darkness such that you cannot even see your hand in front of your face, it is scary. It forces you to think about what you do know. What can you trust? Where are you? But Abram entered this with God. God's voice broke through that darkness. God speaks of things to come. He tells of a future where Abram's children will be enslaved in Egypt for 400 years. Before being brought to this land as HIS Promise to them.

After Abram wakes, he sees God's fire consuming the sacrifice he prepared. Now ask yourself, what was the sign God gave Abram, the vision prophecy, or the consuming of the sacrifice? Maybe it was both.

Dear Lord Jesus,

How is it that You love us so much that You pay attention to my needs and wants? What have I done to deserve Your love and care? I know I have done nothing deserving of it, yet You are there for me. Lord, awaken in me this Love You have for us. Teach me to love as never before. Lord, bring me to a place where I can share Your love for us easier and easier each day!

In Jesus name, Amen.

DAY #46
GENESIS 16:1-6

1   Now Sarai Abram's wife bare him no children: and she had an handmaid, an Egyptian, whose name *was* Hagar.
2   And Sarai said unto Abram, Behold now, the LORD has restrained me from bearing: I pray you, go in unto my maid; it may be that I may obtain children by her. And Abram listened to the voice of Sarai.
3   And Sarai Abram's wife took Hagar her maid the Egyptian, after Abram had dwelt ten years in the land of Canaan, and gave her to her husband Abram to be his wife.
4   And he went in unto Hagar, and she conceived: and when she saw that she had conceived, her mistress was despised in her eyes.
5   And Sarai said unto Abram, My wrong *be* upon you: I have given my maid into your bosom; and when she saw that she

had conceived, I was despised in her eyes: the LORD judge between me and you.

6   But Abram said unto Sarai, Behold, your maid *is* in your hand; do to her as it pleases you. And when Sarai dealt hardly with her, she fled from her face.

Abram loves Sarai so much that he becomes happy just by making her happy. Married men know this feeling of seeing the delight on the faces of their wives because of something they did. But when pleasing your wife, putting that smile on her face, that smile you crave, means doing something you should not, many men still today do not "put their foot down" and say, "No!" Abram, gave in because Sarai was offering her servant to Abram. Today women get paid as Surrogates, but this generally means artificial insemination. Sarai understood the concept of surrogate motherhood. She planned to take the child when it was born and raise it as her own. Abram also seemed to understand that. Even Hagar seemed to grasp the concept – until she was with child. Then the thought of giving up that child was too much. She knew she would have to give her baby to Sarai to raise as her own. She started to despise her mistress. What is interesting and unexpected here is that Sarai's problem is not that Hagar does get pregnant, it is that Sarai suddenly openly despises her. According to the American Heritage Dictionary, despise means to "1. To regard with contempt or scorn. 2. To dislike intensely; loathe. 3'To look down upon with disfavor or contempt; to contemn; to scorn; to disdain; to have a low opinion or contemptuous dislike of."

Hagar would not have been disciplined or kicked out if she did not despise Sarai.

Dear Lord Jesus,

Sometimes us mortals come up with the dumbest of ideas and have to try them. We hear your solution. We see your ideal, but it is not in our timing so we rush and take shortcuts believing it is the only way. LORD, please stop us from trying the shortcuts when we know YOUR WAY is the best and only way we should go. Help us to seek Your love, and not some fake path meant to distract us.

In Jesus name, Amen.

DAY #47
GENESIS 16:7-16

7   And the angel of the LORD found her by a fountain of water in the wilderness, by the fountain in the way to Shur.
8   And he said, Hagar, Sarai's maid, whence came you? and where will you go? And she said, I flee from the face of my mistress Sarai.
9   And the angel of the LORD said unto her, Return to your mistress, and submit yourself under her hands.
10 And the angel of the LORD said unto her, I will multiply your seed exceedingly, that it shall not be numbered for multitude.
11 And the angel of the LORD said unto her, Behold, you *are* with child, and shall bear a son, and shall call his name Ishmael; because the LORD has heard your affliction.
12 And he will be a wild man; his hand *will be* against every man, and every man's hand against him; and he shall dwell in the presence of all his brethren.

13   And she called the name of the LORD that spoke unto her, You God see me: for she said, Have I also here looked after him that sees me?
14   Why the well was called Beerlahairoi; behold, *it is* between Kadesh and Bered.
15   And Hagar bare Abram a son: and Abram called his son's name, which Hagar bare, Ishmael.
16   And Abram *was* fourscore and six years old, when Hagar bare Ishmael to Abram.

Hagar runs from Sarai's discipline. She knows that she ran from the one place, where she can be cared for and looked after. But has to obey her mistress. She is pregnant alone, and some distance away from Abram and Sarai, when who should find her but "an angel of the Lord." "Angel" literally means messenger. This is the first mention of an angel in the Bible. Hagar was first addressed by name and position! Right away, Hagar knows that God is addressing her, because he not only knows her name, she knows her mistress! He knows exactly where she came from and why she is there.

This messenger is likely the Pre-Incarnate image of Jesus, for two reasons. 1) The angel uses "I will multiply your seed." (vs. 10). An angel cannot claim to be God. 2) Hagar even recognizes that this messenger is indeed God incarnate, before her. (Vs. 13) "And she called the name of the LORD that spoke unto her, You God see me."

God sees Hagar! This is the Good Shepherd, who leaves the ninety-nine to seek the lost sheep! How many times do we need to openly admit that God sees all that we do? But for Hagar, it was not only God seeing her, but God showing himself to her. It was something she could not deny. She listens to his words, then returns as she was told, and tells Abram and Sarai what happened. The naming of Ishmael by God, gave her the confidence to return, knowing she would not be harmed. The name Ishmael was given because the LORD had heard Hagar's affliction. What could be done that God would not know? How many more weeks or months she was to be cared for before she delivered the baby is not known. We do know that at the age of eighty-six Abram becomes a father for the first time.

Dear Lord Jesus,

Thank you for all the details you give in your Word of each story so we can know what is true. Even this first recording of a messenger is actually You meeting the maid, Hagar. You show how great a shepherd you are by calling her by name. Lord, we are vain creatures. We like hearing others call our names. But when YOU call our name, there is great joy! Lord, thank you for loving even me.

In Jesus name, Amen.

DAY #48
GENESIS 17:1-14

1   And when Abram was ninety years old and nine, the LORD appeared to Abram, and said unto him, I *am* the Almighty God; walk before me, and be you perfect.

2   And I will make my covenant between me and you, and will multiply you exceedingly.
3   And Abram fell on his face: and God talked with him, saying,
4   As for me, behold, my covenant *is* with you, and you shall be a father of many nations.
5   Neither shall your name any more be called Abram, but your name shall be Abraham; for a father of many nations have I made you.
6   And I will make you exceeding fruitful, and I will make nations of you, and kings shall come out of you.
7   And I will establish my covenant between me and you and your seed after you in their generations for an everlasting covenant, to be a God unto you, and to your seed after you.
8   And I will give unto you, and to your seed after you, the land wherein you are a stranger, all the land of Canaan, for an everlasting possession; and I will be their God.
9   And God said unto Abraham, You shall keep my covenant therefore, you, and your seed after you in their generations.
10 This *is* my covenant, which you shall keep, between me and you and your seed after you; Every man child among you shall be circumcised.
11 And you shall circumcise the flesh of your foreskin; and it shall be a token of the covenant between me and you.
12 And he that is eight days old shall be circumcised among you, every man child in your generations, he that is born in the house, or bought with money of any stranger, which *is* not of your seed.
13 He that is born in your house, and he that is bought with your money, must needs be circumcised: and my covenant shall be in your flesh for an everlasting covenant.

14   And the uncircumcised man child whose flesh of his foreskin is not circumcised, that soul shall be cut off from his people; he has broken my covenant.

God speaks to Abram when he is ninety-nine years old. That is thirteen years after the birth of Ishmael. Even back then Abram was told another child was coming, since his first conversation with God, Abram has known this blessing would come. Now Abram is ready to be blessed with that birth and God changes his name to Abraham. Abraham heard this promise since he was seventy-five! For almost twenty-five years since that promise was given, he has believed that God would do it. Now Abraham is given a process to separate himself and his people, circumcision.

Circumcision can be an extremely painful event for a full-grown man. But, to the eight-day-old male infant, it would not be even a memory. On the eighth day after birth, medical studies have shown a spike in things like Vitamin K that would assist with the healing process. God knew and it took us centuries to figure it out.

Verse 14 is very powerful and sets the stage for many an event yet to happen. This verse tells us that not complying with what God asks in this covenant is the same as cutting yourself off from others who choose to follow God.

Dear Lord Jesus,

Help Abraham heard your promise for twenty-five years. He believed, and waited. What strength. Lord, help me in my unbelief. I fear my faith is not as strong as Abraham's. Help me to be a better example to others of unwavering faith in You and Your love. I have seen You do miracles. I have seen You save people out of horrendous lives. Lord, help me to live a holy life. Help me to be a stronger person in You so that others may see YOUR love.

In Jesus name, Amen.

DAY #49
GENESIS 17:15-20

15   And God said unto Abraham, As for Sarai your wife, you shall not call her name Sarai, but Sarah *shall* her name *be*.
16   And I will bless her, and give you a son also of her: yea, I will bless her, and she shall be *a mother* of nations; kings of people shall be of her.
17   Then Abraham fell upon his face, and laughed, and said in his heart, Shall *a child* be born unto him that is an hundred years old? and shall Sarah, that is ninety years old, bear?
18   And Abraham said unto God, O that Ishmael might live before you!
19   And God said, Sarah your wife shall bear you a son indeed; and you shall call his name Isaac: and I will establish my covenant with him for an everlasting covenant, *and* with his seed after him.
20   And as for Ishmael, I have heard you: Behold, I have blessed him, and will make him fruitful, and will multiply him exceedingly; twelve princes shall he beget, and I will make him a great nation.

This laughter of Abraham is often misattributed to Sarah. He laughs because he knows that a certain stage of life women go through menopause and children are an impossibility. Sarah was far past that. Abraham had faith in God's promise, but was somehow forgetting he was talking with God, who does impossible things. He believed in a promise, but not in God to fulfill it as he claimed? The best thing about this passage is that it shows it is ok to have doubts about God and His ability. God does not care about that, what he cares about is the relationship you have with him. The relationship should grow. Just as a husband and wife grow old and can often finish each other's sentences, your relationship with God should grow and you should know what it is he wants for you, and your belief should grow enabling you to say, "My God does impossible things!"

Abraham pushed his son Ishmael as a possible fulfillment, the one made through a relationship not with his wife, but with her servant. God listened. "I have heard you…" What an incredible thing to hear from God who does impossible things. Think about this. It means Abraham has access to the miracle maker! It also means that because of Abraham Ishmael gets another blessing besides what was promised to Hagar. These blessings still are not promises made to Ishmael but to his parents.

Dear Lord Jesus,

Some people foolishly insist you are not God. Yet, You brought the dead to life. You were before Abraham, and you were the very person that blessed Abram with the name Abraham. Lord, open our eyes, help us to see the many blessings you grant each day, despite our own foolishness. Lord, I know You won't give up on us and

You will continue to mold and make us after Your will. Lord, help us to grow in our relationship with You, now more than ever.

In Jesus name, Amen.

DAY #50
GENESIS 17:21-27

21 But my covenant will I establish with Isaac, which Sarah shall bear unto you at this set time in the next year.
22 And he left off talking with him, and God went up from Abraham.
23 And Abraham took Ishmael his son, and all that were born in his house, and all that were bought with his money, every male among the men of Abraham's house; and circumcised the flesh of their foreskin in the selfsame day, as God had said unto him.
24 And Abraham *was* ninety years old and nine, when he was circumcised in the flesh of his foreskin.
25 And Ishmael his son *was* thirteen years old, when he was circumcised in the flesh of his foreskin.
26 In the selfsame day was Abraham circumcised, and Ishmael his son.
27 And all the men of his house, born in the house, and bought with money of the stranger, were circumcised with him.

Ishmael has no covenant made with him. The promises granted to him are based on who his father and mother are. They have nothing to do with who he becomes. Isaac, who has yet to be born, is promised a covenant one year before he is born.

Verse 22 reveals Abraham was right in thinking this was God NOT an angel, "… and God went up from Abraham."

Now it is all on Abraham to be obedient. He has to get circumcised at the age of ninety-nine! Not only him but all the males on the very day he spoke with God! Abraham felt there could be no delay in this action. There was a need to rush to have no chance of being cut off from God.

The pain of circumcision would have been excruciating considering the lack of painkillers outside of alcohol. Abraham had to have a clue about the pain, and still, he rushed to get this done. Those men that were with him, followed him willingly even if hesitantly into this. What kind of a presence and influential talent must Abraham have had if they all just followed?

An interesting note here differentiates between servants and slaves, " … and bought with the money the stranger." Male slaves seem to have been given to Abraham as either gifts or payment. But Abraham himself, nor any of those with him, bought them. The money spent was that of a stranger. Those who served were employed in some manner.

Dear Lord Jesus,

How often do You tell us to do something and we simply push it aside? I know for me that is too easy. Would I have rushed to make sure I did not get cut off from You? Even though the thought of being cut off from You is horrible, I cannot say I would rush into pain to be obedient as Abraham was on this day. Lord, keep working on me. I am nowhere close to Abraham rushing to obey

You on that day. Lord, I want to be like Abraham, one who rushes to do Your will.

In Jesus name, Amen.

DAY #51
GENESIS 18:1-15

1 And the LORD appeared unto him in the plains of Mamre: and he sat in the tent door in the heat of the day;
2 And he lift up his eyes and looked, and, lo, three men stood by him: and when he saw *them*, he ran to meet them from the tent door, and bowed himself toward the ground,
3 And said, My Lord, if now I have found favour in your sight, pass not away, I pray you, from your servant:
4 Let a little water, I pray you, be fetched, and wash your feet, and rest yourselves under the tree:
5 And I will fetch a morsel of bread, and comfort you your hearts; after that you shall pass on: for therefore are you come to your servant. And they said, So do, as you have said.
6 And Abraham *have*ened into the tent unto Sarah, and said, Make ready quickly three measures of fine meal, knead *it*, and make cakes upon the hearth.
7 And Abraham ran unto the herd, and fetched a calf tender and good, and gave *it* unto a young man; and he *have*ed to dress it.
8 And he took butter, and milk, and the calf which he had dressed, and set *it* before them; and he stood by them under the tree, and they did eat.

9   And they said unto him, Where *is* Sarah your wife? And he said, Behold, in the tent.
10 And he said, I will certainly return unto you according to the time of life; and, lo, Sarah your wife shall have a son. And Sarah heard *it* in the tent door, which *was* behind him.
11 Now Abraham and Sarah *were* old *and* well stricken in age; *and* it ceased to be with Sarah after the manner of women.
12 Therefore Sarah laughed within herself, saying, After I am waxed old shall I have pleasure, my lord being old also?
13 And the LORD said unto Abraham, Why did Sarah laugh, saying, Shall I of a surety bear a child, which am old?
14 Is any thing too hard for the LORD? At the time appointed I will return unto you, according to the time of life, and Sarah shall have a son.
15 Then Sarah denied, saying, I laughed not; for she was afraid. And he said, Nay; but you *did* laugh.

Of the three men present Abraham immediately recognizes GOD in the flesh, this is the pre-incarnate image of Christ! Abraham had seen God before. Abraham knew HIM, and like before he is compelled to rush and serve HIM. He ran to meet HIM (a short distance), then rushed to get the best food he could offer. There is a need for Abraham not to impress, but to give his absolute best to God.

Sarah laughs when she hears God's promise of her carrying a child. No matter how many times she has heard this promise from Abraham, and probably heard his own admission at laughing at God's promise, she can't help but laugh at the impossibility of herself bearing a child at her age. It is truly a loving couple that reflect each other's thoughts. Abraham had just laughed at the exact same thing in 17:17. Sarah however foolishly in the presence of God denied this. God needed her to see HE can do the impossible. Sometimes we have to express our disbelief in order to grow past it. Remember that Isaac earned his name from his father's laughter first.

Think about this time God spent with Abraham and Sarah as you do when a friend is on a business trip and has to stop nearby. Your friend will stop and visit. This is an act of love and caring. It is an act of maintaining a friendship. Such a visit is unnecessary and at the same time necessary, because we desire the closeness of those we love. God loved Abraham. He was "passing through on business." This seems somewhat silly, to think of God visiting while on a business trip. Yet, God came and saw Abraham at the door of his tent, and was on his way to deal with the sins of Sodom and Gomorrah as we shall see tomorrow. This visit is an expression of love, it is an expression of maintaining a relationship not only with Abraham, but with his wife Sarah.

Dear Lord Jesus,

How is it that You love us so, when we so easily put You aside to do things we know are wrong. Lord, You know us so well. You teach us to love through all You do. You teach us about relationships and the importance of being there in person. Lord, help me to become that example You desire of me. Help me to show Your love so others may find Your love.

In Jesus name, Amen.

DAY #52
GENESIS 18:16-33

16 And the men rose up from there, and looked toward Sodom: and Abraham went with them to bring them on the way.
17 And the LORD said, Shall I hide from Abraham that thing which I do;
18 Seeing that Abraham shall surely become a great and mighty nation, and all the nations of the earth shall be blessed in him?
19 For I know him, that he will command his children and his household after him, and they shall keep the way of the LORD, to do justice and judgment; that the LORD may bring upon Abraham that which he has spoken of him.
20 And the LORD said, Because the cry of Sodom and Gomorrah is great, and because their sin is very grievous;
21 I will go down now, and see whether they have done altogether according to the cry of it, which is come unto me; and if not, I will know.
22 And the men turned their faces from there, and went toward Sodom: but Abraham stood yet before the LORD.
23 And Abraham drew near, and said, Will you also destroy the righteous with the wicked?
24 Peradventure there be fifty righteous within the city: will you also destroy and not spare the place for the fifty righteous that *are* therein?
25 That be far from you to do after this manner, to slay the righteous with the wicked: and that the righteous should be as the wicked, that be far from you: Shall not the Judge of all the earth do right?
26 And the LORD said, If I find in Sodom fifty righteous within the city, then I will spare all the place for their sakes.

27 And Abraham answered and said, Behold now, I have taken upon me to speak unto the Lord, which *am but* dust and ashes:

28 Peradventure there shall lack five of the fifty righteous: will you destroy all the city for *lack of* five? And he said, If I find there forty and five, I will not destroy *it*.

29 And he spoke unto him yet again, and said, Peradventure there shall be forty found there. And he said, I will not do *it* for forty's sake.

30 And he said *unto him*, Oh let not the Lord be angry, and I will speak: Peradventure there shall thirty be found there. And he said, I will not do *it*, if I find thirty there.

31 And he said, Behold now, I have taken upon me to speak unto the Lord: Peradventure there shall be twenty found there. And he said, I will not destroy *it* for twenty's sake.

32 And he said, Oh let not the Lord be angry, and I will speak yet but this once: Peradventure ten shall be found there. And he said, I will not destroy *it* for ten's sake.

33 And the LORD went his way, as soon as he had left communing with Abraham: and Abraham returned unto his place.

Abraham asked, God if he would "destroy the righteous with the wicked." He did this knowing where Lot, his nephew, his dead brother's son, lived – in Sodom. If Lot, kept just a few with him and continued to live according to the example he set, maybe just maybe Lot would be ok. God knew Abraham was asking if he would at least spare his nephew. But Abraham did not mention his name. This may have been based on Abraham himself not having confidence his nephew's ability to stay away from sin.

This question Abraham poses is important, because Islam's god, has no problem with "destroying the righteous with the wicked." Their god does not protect those that follow him. This is why we known their God is not of an Abrahamic faith! That god is too small.

The God of Abraham, was willing to tell Abraham about what HE was going to do, and wanted to have Abraham ask these questions. God was willing to talk about this with Abraham in person! This is another example of how much God loves us. He wanted to keep Abraham informed, and he wanted Abraham to know, YAWEH, the LIVING GOD, does NOT destroy the righteous with the wicked.

Dear Lord Jesus,

You were there face to face with Abraham. You spoke to him and explained to him that You are the RIGHTEOUS ONE. You go out of your way to show us that YOU are the God who loved us first. How is it You love us so much, even though we do not deserve it at all? Lord, please keep working on me. I want to be a better example of Your love each day. Lord, use me to bring others to know Your precious love.

In Jesus name, Amen.

DAY #53
GENESIS 19:1-14

1 And there came two angels to Sodom at even; and Lot sat in the gate of Sodom: and Lot seeing *them* rose up to meet them; and he bowed himself with his face toward the ground;

2 And he said, Behold now, my lords, turn in, I pray you, into your servant's house, and tarry all night, and wash your feet, and you shall rise up early, and go on your ways. And they said, Nay; but we will abide in the street all night.

3 And he pressed upon them greatly; and they turned in unto him, and entered into his house; and he made them a feast, and did bake unleavened bread, and they did eat.

4 But before they lay down, the men of the city, *even* the men of Sodom, compassed the house round, both old and young, all the people from every quarter:

5 And they called unto Lot, and said unto him, Where *are* the men which came in to you this night? bring them out unto us, that we may know them.

6 And Lot went out at the door unto them, and shut the door after him,

7 And said, I pray you, brethren, do not so wickedly.

8 Behold now, I have two daughters which have not known man; let me, I pray you, bring them out unto you, and do you to them as *is* good in your eyes: only unto these men do nothing; for therefore came they under the shadow of my roof.

9 And they said, Stand back. And they said *again*, This one *fellow* came in to sojourn, and he will needs be a judge: now will we deal worse with you, than with them. And they pressed sore upon the man, *even* Lot, and came near to break the door.

10 But the men put forth their hand, and pulled Lot into the house to them, and shut to the door.
11 And they smote the men that *were* at the door of the house with blindness, both small and great: so that they wearied themselves to find the door.
12 And the men said unto Lot, Have you here any besides? son in law, and your sons, and your daughters, and whatsoever you have in the city, bring *them* out of this place:
13 For we will destroy this place, because the cry of them is waxen great before the face of the LORD; and the LORD has sent us to destroy it.
14 And Lot went out, and spoke unto his sons in law, which married his daughters, and said, Up, get you out of this place; for the LORD will destroy this city. But he seemed as one that mocked unto his sons in law.

 This was the day God sent his two angels into Sodom. Lot recognizes immediately that these are not normal men, but angels of the living God, that his uncle Abraham serves. Lot knew that Abraham served God. He was around when miracles happened. He saw undeniable blessings and still did not seem to pursue God on his own when he was parted from his uncle. Lot saw these men as holy, pure, and needing protection. What a foolish mistake. He saw GOD as one of those many little gods he knew of where he grew up. They were only capable of certain things and had limits to their powers.

 Lot was such a fool he was willing to toss away his daughters to protect the angels. That is the one thing that should anger every father! What kind of man was Lot, that he would willingly sacrifice them? He was the type of man who would marry his daughters off to men who cared not for God without a worry. This part of the story reveals how self-serving Lot in truth was. For Lot was a man who offered his own daughters up.

The angels proved that God was far better than Lot comprehended. They would not allow someone's innocence to be sacrificed for them.

Note that Lot has gone from a man of great wealth. A man whose possessions and greatness were known, down to living unprotected in a city where such violence and rampant deviance were considered the norm. He had been saved by his uncle and his men once. Now angels have come and he presses them to come into his house "to protect them?" This was a man who would not protect his own daughters. Lot was not a righteous man at all.

Dear Lord Jesus,

You bless even those who surround those who love You. You give us many opportunities to recognize who YOU are and still so many of us won't open our own eyes to the things You have done to show us Your love. Lord, remove from me the silence and fear that hold my voice back. Today, use me to speak boldly of this incredible love You have so one more person can hear of your precious love expressed on the cross for us.

In Jesus name, Amen.

DAY #54
GENESIS 19:15-29

15 And when the morning arose, then the angels *have*ened Lot, saying, Arise, take your wife, and your two daughters, which are here; lest you be consumed in the iniquity of the city.
16 And while he lingered, the men laid hold upon his hand, and upon the hand of his wife, and upon the hand of his two daughters; the LORD being merciful unto him: and they brought him forth, and set him without the city.
17 And it came to pass, when they had brought them forth abroad, that he said, Escape for your life; look not behind you, neither stay you in all the plain; escape to the mountain, lest you be consumed.
18 And Lot said unto them, Oh, not so, my Lord:
19 Behold now, your servant has found grace in your sight, and you have magnified your mercy, which you have shown unto me in saving my life; and I cannot escape to the mountain, lest some evil take me, and I die:
20 Behold now, this city *is* near to flee unto, and it *is* a little one: Oh, let me escape there, (*is* it not a little one?) and my soul shall live.
21 And he said unto him, See, I have accepted you concerning this thing also, that I will not overthrow this city, for the which you have spoken.
22 *Have*e you, escape there; for I cannot do any thing till you get there. Therefore the name of the city was called Zoar.
23 The sun was risen upon the earth when Lot entered into Zoar.

What does it mean when a man is told to rush and leave the city for it will be abolished, it will feel the hand of God for its love of sin, and that man "lingers?" He should be rushing his wife and two youngest daughters to pack and flee. But Lot, the one who is supposed to be leading the family, is leading them in lingering. Yes, his grown daughters and son-in-laws will soon face the wrath of God, but he tried to reach them and they laughed at him as if he was a foolish old man who had lost his faculties. There was no resemblance of respect or deference to an elder. This is the type of community Lot chose to live in, and the place he thought was good to raise his children? Now, he is the one and only person whose family is blessed with deliverance from the coming punishment from God on this city and he is not *hastening*? In fact, his lingering and that of his wife and daughters is so noticed that the angels lay hold of their wrists and physically remove them from the city, pulling them. These are not the actions of a righteous man. But it gets worse. Having been taken out of the city, one of the angels says, "Escape for your life; look not behind you, neither stay you in all the plain; escape to the mountain, lest you be consumed." I don't know about you, but at that point, I would be telling my family to hold hands and start running! But Lot and his family---. Lot starts to "negotiate." This makes Lot the exact opposite of Abraham, who ran to meet God, who rushed to give his best. Lot drags himself resisting doing what is right, not only for himself, but for his family. Then tries to talk his way out of what is next. He was told to flee to the mountains but negotiates his move to another city, which is thought to be just 5 miles away.

An average human walks 3 miles an hour. Lot and his family only had to walk for less than two hours. If they ran as much as they could, that would be a lot less time! Lot takes about four hours to get there! This is the reason God told Abraham to leave Lot behind in the beginning. It is the reason God waited until Lot was parted from Abraham to bless him.

Which is the man you would willingly follow, Abraham a man who rushes to do whatever God asks, or Lot a man who lingers and delays doing what God asks?

Dear Lord Jesus,

How is it that you love us so much that even when we are such sinners you seek us out to deliver us from evil? You had Abram separate himself from Lot, so he could be blessed. Yet because of Your love of Abraham, You even protected his loved nephew. Lord, hear me, I have many I know that need to find Your love. Send many to them until they discover Your love.

In Jesus' name, Amen.

DAY #55
GENESIS 19:23-38

23   The sun was risen upon the earth when Lot entered into Zoar.
24   Then the LORD rained upon Sodom and upon Gomorrah brimstone and fire from the LORD out of heaven;
25   And he overthrew those cities, and all the plain, and all the inhabitants of the cities, and that which grew upon the ground.
26   But his wife looked back from behind him, and she became a pillar of salt.
27   And Abraham gat up early in the morning to the place where he stood before the LORD:

28 And he looked toward Sodom and Gomorrah, and toward all the land of the plain, and beheld, and, lo, the smoke of the country went up as the smoke of a furnace.

29 And it came to pass, when God destroyed the cities of the plain, that God remembered Abraham, and sent Lot out of the midst of the overthrow, when he overthrew the cities in the which Lot dwelt.

30 And Lot went up out of Zoar, and dwelt in the mountain, and his two daughters with him; for he feared to dwell in Zoar: and he dwelt in a cave, he and his two daughters.

31 And the firstborn said unto the younger, Our father *is* old, and *There is* not a man in the earth to come in unto us after the manner of all the earth:

32 Come, let us make our father drink wine, and we will lie with him, that we may preserve seed of our father.

33 And they made their father drink wine that night: and the firstborn went in, and lay with her father; and he perceived not when she lay down, nor when she arose.

34 And it came to pass on the morrow, that the firstborn said unto the younger, Behold, I lay yesternight with my father: let us make him drink wine this night also; and go you in, *and* lie with him, that we may preserve seed of our father.

35 And they made their father drink wine that night also: and the younger arose, and lay with him; and he perceived not when she lay down, nor when she arose.

36 Thus were both the daughters of Lot with child by their father.

37 And the firstborn bare a son, and called his name Moab: the same *is* the father of the Moabites unto this day.

38 And the younger, she also bare a son, and called his name Benammi: the same *is* the father of the children of Ammon unto this day.

Lot, the unrighteous man, was saved because of his uncle's love for him, not once but twice. This time Abraham's love for his nephew, though knowing of what evils he may be engaged in, has reached the Lord God himself, and HE has sent angels to preserve not only Lot's life but that of his household. What does this say about God's love for the lost, that HE would intervene for such an unworthy man as Lot. A man who would not only not protect his own daughters from harm, but would sacrifice them for the safety of strangers.

Sin comes with horrible penalties. Especially those made in the raising of children. Lot's children do not trust him. They have no faith in their father telling the truth. They think he is nothing but an old man with a wild imagination. He has not taught them about God. He has not taught them about the miracles he saw when he was with his uncle. Worse, he has raised them to be indifferent to the sexual promiscuity in the world around them. He has not set a standard of right and wrong for his family. Because of this, Lot's penalty is one of legacy. His name bears the shame of foolishness and incest.

Dear Lord Jesus,

You know my sins, my own foolishness, please forgive me. Lord, YOU set my feet on the solid ground of Your Word! Lord, awaken in me a fervor to reach not only the lost but their families. Use me, Lord, to draw others to You so that their families may see a change and growth in the wonders of Your work changing us from the inside. Lord, YOU do impossible things. I ask that You use me to plant seeds so others may see this change You cause within them.

In Jesus name, Amen.

DAY #56
GENESIS 20:1-18

1   And Abraham journeyed from there toward the south country, and dwelled between Kadesh and Shur, and sojourned in Gerar.
2   And Abraham said of Sarah his wife, She *is* my sister: and Abimelech king of Gerar sent, and took Sarah.
3   But God came to Abimelech in a dream by night, and said to him, Behold, you *are but* a dead man, for the woman which you have taken; for she *is* a man's wife.
4   But Abimelech had not come near her: and he said, Lord, will you slay also a righteous nation?
5   Said he not unto me, She *is* my sister? and she, even she herself said, He *is* my brother: in the integrity of my heart and innocency of my hands have I done this.
6   And God said unto him in a dream, Yea, I know that you did this in the integrity of your heart; for I also withheld you from sinning against me: therefore suffered I you not to touch her.
7   Now therefore restore the man *his* wife; for he *is* a prophet, and he shall pray for you, and you shall live: and if you restore *her* not, know you that you shall surely die, you, and all that *are* your.
8   Therefore Abimelech rose early in the morning, and called all his servants, and told all these things in their ears: and the men were sore afraid.
9   Then Abimelech called Abraham, and said unto him, What have you done unto us? and what have I offended you, that

you have brought on me and on my kingdom a great sin? you have done deeds unto me that ought not to be done.

10   And Abimelech said unto Abraham, What did you see, that you have done this thing?

11   nd Abraham said, Because I thought, Surely the fear of God *is* not in this place; and they will slay me for my wife's sake.

12   And yet indeed [she is] my sister; she *is* the daughter of my father, but not the daughter of my mother; and she became my wife.

13   And it came to pass, when God caused me to wander from my father's house, that I said unto her, This *is* your kindness which you shall show unto me; at every place where we shall come, say of me, He *is* my brother.

14   And Abimelech took sheep, and oxen, and menservants, and women-servants, and gave *them* unto Abraham, and restored him Sarah his wife.

15   And Abimelech said, Behold, my land *is* before you: dwell where it pleases you.

16   And unto Sarah he said, Behold, I have given your brother a thousand *pieces* of silver: behold, he *is* to you a covering of the eyes, unto all that *are* with you, and with all *other*: thus she was reproved.

17   So Abraham prayed unto God: and God healed Abimelech, and his wife, and his maidservants; and they bare *children*.

18   For the LORD had fast closed up all the wombs of the house of Abimelech, because of Sarah Abraham's wife.

This seems like a repetition of a sin Abraham committed earlier. "Seems" is the right description. Instead, because Abimelech was not a man with a lustful mindset and was a man who did fear

God, we learn the backstory too much of Abraham's foolishness and long wait for the blessing of a child from God. Abraham had married his half-sister. He made a pact with his wife, AFTER God spoke to him, to conceal her being married to him, if his life should be in danger. Abraham trusted Sarah to protect him more than God! This secret sin of Abraham had to be dealt with, it had to be addressed before he and Sarah could be blessed. Here it is confessed, and Abraham instead of being driven out for causing problems like he was from Egypt, Abimelech blesses Abraham and offers him a place to stay.

Abraham had done one other thing to get into this spot. Abraham had left the area God said he and his children would be given. Knowing that, Abraham could not stay, but he gained a powerful ally. God introduced Abraham as a prophet to Abimelech. Abraham does talk with God easily, so he is asked to pray to open the wombs of Abimelech's household. He does this and the women give birth. At first glance, it appears that this means Abraham did not rush off. He stayed at least nine months, but as we learn in the next chapter, it means Abraham and Sarah conceived the very day God visited. It means that Abraham and she had to have visited and left while she was still not showing her pregnancy. It also means that Abraham continued to be in contact with Abimelech after he and Sarah left.

Think about this passage and ask yourself, "Am I holding God back from blessing me?"

Dear Lord Jesus,

My own sinfulness holds me back from what You desire to bless me with. This is a hard lesson. It is not easy to hear. Yet it makes more sense than I care to admit. Lord, I know I need You to change me more and more each day. I want to grow in YOU and become a better person each day. Help me to put away my sinfulness. Help me to see the strength that is in Your WORD, to fight back, and keep me on Your path.

In Jesus name, Amen.

DAY #57
GENESIS 21:1-14

1 And the LORD visited Sarah as he had said, and the LORD did unto Sarah as he had spoken.
2 For Sarah conceived, and bare Abraham a son in his old age, at the set time of which God had spoken to him.
3 And Abraham called the name of his son that was born unto him, whom Sarah bare to him, Isaac.
4 And Abraham circumcised his son Isaac being eight days old, as God had commanded him.
5 And Abraham was an hundred years old, when his son Isaac was born unto him.
6 And Sarah said, God has made me to laugh, *so that* all that hear will laugh with me.
7 And she said, Who would have said unto Abraham, that Sarah should have given children suck? for I have born *him* a son in his old age.
8 And the child grew, and was weaned: and Abraham made a great feast the *same* day that Isaac was weaned.
9 And Sarah saw the son of Hagar the Egyptian, which she had born unto Abraham, mocking.

10   Why she said unto Abraham, Cast out this bondwoman and her son: for the son of this bondwoman shall not be heir with my son, *even* with Isaac.
11   And the thing was very grievous in Abraham's sight because of his son.
12   And God said unto Abraham, Let it not be grievous in your sight because of the lad, and because of your bondwoman; in all that Sarah has said unto you, listen unto her voice; for in Isaac shall your seed be called.
13   And also of the son of the bondwoman will I make a nation, because he *is* your seed.
14   And Abraham rose up early in the morning, and took bread, and a bottle of water, and gave *it* unto Hagar, putting *it* on her shoulder, and the child, and sent her away: and she departed, and wandered in the wilderness of Beersheba.

When God spoke to Abraham again of the promise of Isaac, as much as both Abraham and Sarah laughed at the idea of her giving birth in her old age, the two that day gave it a chance. That day according to this passage Sarah conceived. This means that during the time she was at Abimelech's, she was not yet showing.

Abraham was obedient and circumcised Isaac on the eighth day. Then when the time of weaning came they held a celebration. This celebration was about surviving at the high infant mortality rate. At that celebration, Ishmael is caught mocking Isaac. But the way it is communicated in the scripture implicates that Ishmael was copying something he heard his mother say. What is problematic here is that Ishmael was by now a young adult. Hagar's choice to be rebellious to Sarah and Isaac had grown to the point it must be dealt with. Sarah brings the problem to her husband Abraham. Abraham wants peace, he doesn't want his son, Ishmael, sent away, so he seeks God. God tells him it is ok to send them off. Abraham, then does what God says is right.

It is important not to miss that Abraham did not want this, but God approved of it. It is also important to grasp that Abraham and Sarah did not put Ishmael's sin on him but on his mother. This should make us think about what behaviors we are teaching our children through what we say and do.

Dear Lord Jesus,

I shudder to think what willful separation of family means. Whether it be a divorce, separation, or whatever reason, it always hurts. You are there for us during these hard times. We may not grasp that at the moment. We may feel all alone, but YOU were there holding our hands through it all. Lord, help us to stop thinking so much about how life impacts us and our selfish needs. Help us to see what You see as needed for us to do.

In Jesus name, Amen.

DAY #57
GENESIS 21:15-21

15 And the water was spent in the bottle, and she cast the child under one of the shrubs.
16 And she went, and sat her down over against *him* a good way off, as it were a bowshot: for she said, Let me not see

the death of the child. And she sat over against *him*, and lift up her voice, and wept.

17 And God heard the voice of the lad; and the angel of God called to Hagar out of heaven, and said unto her, What ails you, Hagar? fear not; for God has heard the voice of the lad where he *is*.

18 Arise, lift up the lad, and hold him in your hand; for I will make him a great nation.

19 And God opened her eyes, and she saw a well of water; and she went, and filled the bottle with water, and gave the lad drink.

20 And God was with the lad; and he grew, and dwelt in the wilderness, and became an archer.

21 And he dwelt in the wilderness of Paran: and his mother took him a wife out of the land of Egypt.

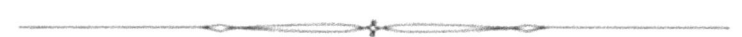

The story of Hagar running out of water seems almost as if she is playing the drama queen again. But mothers think of their children, even if they are young adults. If she has no water that is one thing. She cries out to God, but GOD does not hear her. God hears Ishmael's cries for water! This shows God knows us all too well. Whether we are all about the drama, or about what is real, God knows. God had already told Hagar her son was blessed. Why did she not go forward believing? Keep in mind she will continue to influence Ishmael with her lack of faith.

Ishmael was circumcised when he was thirteen! Yet, this story is about three years later. Part of the purpose of digging deeper into God's Word is getting at the truth, finding out more than the things that can be easily missed. As Ishmael was a young adult, why is it God heard his cries for water, but responded not to him, but to his mother? God had blessed Ishmael for his father Abraham's love.

But it is apparent that Ishmael has not chosen to follow his father Abraham's example of love for his God.

People often call Islam an Abrahamic faith believing that Ishmael was served the same God as his father Abraham. They forget his mother raised him, and that she went back to Egypt to get him a wife. These women were used to worshipping many gods. Ishmael may have been Abraham's son, but his faith was not close to that of his father.

Dear Lord Jesus,

You do amazing things! You listen to us beg and plead for what could be the smallest of things, and that makes you happy because we are communicating with You. Help me to dig deeper into Your Word that I may know You better. Lord change me into someone better. Make me more loving and more understanding.

In Jesus name, Amen.

DAY #58
GENESIS 21:22-34

22 And it came to pass at that time, that Abimelech and Phichol the chief captain of his host spoke unto Abraham, saying, God *is* with you in all that you do:
23 Now therefore swear unto me here by God that you will not deal falsely with me, nor with my son, nor with my son's son: *but* according to the kindness that I have done unto

	you, you shall do unto me, and to the land wherein you *have* sojourned.
24	And Abraham said, I will swear.
25	And Abraham reproved Abimelech because of a well of water, which Abimelech's servants had violently taken away.
26	And Abimelech said, I do not *know* who has done this thing: neither *did* you tell me, neither yet heard I *of it*, but to day.
27	And Abraham took sheep and oxen, and gave them unto Abimelech; and both of them made a covenant.
28	And Abraham set seven ewe lambs of the flock by themselves.
29	And Abimelech said unto Abraham, What *mean* these seven ewe lambs which you *have* set by themselves?
30	And he said, For *these* seven ewe lambs shall you take of my hand, that they may be a witness unto me, that I have dug this well.
31	Why he called that place Beersheba; because there they swore both of them.
32	Thus they made a covenant at Beersheba: then Abimelech rose up, and Phichol the chief captain of his host, and they returned into the land of the Philistines.
33	And *Abraham* planted a grove in Beersheba, and called there on the name of the LORD, the everlasting God.
34	And Abraham sojourned in the Philistines' land many days.

The way this passage sits here actually brings less significance to Hagar and Ishmael leaving, and greater significance to this meeting. Here Abimielech initiates a meeting with Abraham to not just stay in a good relationship, but to create a treaty that would last generations. Abimelech comes with his head of the army. This could have been a show of force, it could also have been Abimelech's way of teaching his general not to mess with Abraham. They are in the land of the Philistines which is significant in that this land is to become part of the Promised Land!

This treaty/covenant is sworn on God. This is interesting because it seems a one-way treaty. Yet, this treaty is immediately used by Abraham to call on Abimelech "to act honestly." He was "kept in the dark," in respect to what his men had done. Then he was also put on the spot having to recognize and acknowledge the well made by Abraham. This well may seem somewhat insignificant, but its location is indeed a statement.

Dear Lord Jesus,

You are the worker of miracles. You put us in positions to ask for Your miraculous intervention to help others. Lord, You give us access to miracles! A pact may not seem like a miracle today, but this pact is important. Lord thank you for preserving Your WORD!

In Jesus name, Amen.

DAY #59
GENESIS 22:1-19

1   And it came to pass after these things, that God did tempt Abraham, and said unto him, Abraham: and he said, Behold, *here* I *am*.

2   And he said, Take now your son, your only *son* Isaac, whom you love, and get you into the land of Moriah; and offer him there for a burnt offering upon one of the mountains which I will tell you of.

3   And Abraham rose up early in the morning, and saddled his ass, and took two of his young men with him, and Isaac his son, and clave the wood for the burnt offering, and rose up, and went unto the place of which God had told him.

4   Then on the third day Abraham lifted up his eyes, and saw the place afar off.

5   And Abraham said unto his young men, Abide you here with the ass; and I and the lad will go yonder and worship, and come again to you.

6   And Abraham took the wood of the burnt offering, and laid *it* upon Isaac his son; and he took the fire in his hand, and a knife; and they went both of them together.

7   And Isaac spoke unto Abraham his father, and said, My father: and he said, Here *am* I, my son. And he said, Behold the fire and the wood: but where *is* the lamb for a burnt offering?

8   And Abraham said, My son, God will provide himself a lamb for a burnt offering: so they went both of them together.

9   And they came to the place which God had told him of; and Abraham built an altar there, and laid the wood in order, and bound Isaac his son, and laid him on the altar upon the wood.

10   And Abraham stretched forth his hand, and took the knife to slay his son.

11   And the angel of the LORD called unto him out of heaven, and said, Abraham, Abraham: and he said, Here *am* I.

12   And he said, Lay not your hand upon the lad, neither do you any thing unto him: for now I know that you fear God,

seeing you *have* not withheld your son, your only *son* from me.

13   And Abraham lifted up his eyes, and looked, and behold behind *him* a ram caught in a thicket by his horns: and Abraham went and took the ram, and offered him up for a burnt offering in the place of his son.

14   And Abraham called the name of that place Jehovahjireh: as it is said *to* this day, In the mount of the LORD it shall be seen.

15   And the angel of the LORD called unto Abraham out of heaven the second time,

16   And said, By myself have I sworn, says the LORD, for because you *have* done this thing, and *have* not withheld your son, your only *son*:

17   That in blessing I will bless you, and in multiplying I will multiply your seed as the stars of the heaven, and as the sand which *is* upon the sea shore; and your seed shall possess the gate of his enemies;

18   And in your seed shall all the nations of the earth be blessed; because you *have* obeyed my voice.

19   So Abraham returned unto his young men, and they rose up and went together to Beersheba; and Abraham dwelt at Beersheba.

Abraham was not unfamiliar with human sacrifices. They had them in Ur[1] before he left. Here he was with the son God had promised him, and the promise was also extended to Isaac's children. How could God make such a promise, leave it seemingly unfulfilled for so long, and now after the child is growing to manhood, ask for that child back? For Abraham, the answer only had one

---

[1] (Hassett & Sağlamtimur, 2018)

possibility. He was willing to obey but believed it to be a test. He told his son as much when he went up to the place where he gave the sacrifice. God does not go back on HIS word! Isaac was testimony of that! How could a woman past childbearing age and a 100-year-old man have a child? Yet, here he was – Isaac was all too real! He was a living testimony of God doing the impossible! So, if Abraham believed God, and God still required the life of his child – he believed Isaac would be resurrected. After all, God was and is the best promise keeper!

Dear Lord Jesus!

YOU ARE THE GREAT AND MIGHTY MIRACLE WORKER! How can we give up knowing that you grant us access to miracles? Lord, work on us, mold us, and make us more like you, that we might stand, bold and daring when standing on YOUR WORD!

In Jesus name, Amen.

DAY #60
GENESIS 22:20-24

20   And it came to pass after these things, that it was told Abraham, saying, Behold, Milcah, she has also born children unto your brother Nahor;
21   Huz his firstborn, and Buz his brother, and Kemuel the father of Aram,

22   And Chesed, and Hazo, and Pildash, and Jidlaph, and Bethuel.
23   And Bethuel begat Rebekah: these eight Milcah did bear to Nahor, Abraham's brother.
24   And his concubine, whose name *was* Reumah, she bare also Tebah, and Gaham, and Thahash, and Maachah.

This passage may seem insignificant, maybe to some, it seems unimportant. But this passage explains Rebekah's lineage. Rebekah is to be Isaac's wife. We learn here that Isaac's future wife is his second cousin.

When you think about this, why was it that all these eight children and their children were not announced to Abraham before? The reason for this was that Abraham chose to share his joyous celebration of his son Isaac's coming of age with them. His silent brother, who also is still alive like a true brother shares his own joys in his eight children and grandchildren. This news becomes of great importance. Because Isaac is old enough to marry. Where should he look for a Godly woman? This is an important conversation as that task, that job, fell not to Isaac but to his parents to help him find such a woman. God's plan for Isaac is just beginning!

Dear Lord Jesus,

In Your Word, it says, "it is not good that man should be alone." You provide answers to our needs and wants before we even know them. You know our hearts! Lord, keep us seeking YOU first, so that we may be the men and women You desire us to be!

In Jesus name, Amen.

DAY #61
GENESIS 23:1-20

1   And Sarah was an hundred and seven and twenty years old: *these were* the years of the life of Sarah.
2   And Sarah died in Kirjatharba; the same *is* Hebron in the land of Canaan: and Abraham came to mourn for Sarah, and to weep for her.
3   And Abraham stood up from before his dead, and spoke unto the sons of Heth, saying,
4   I *am* a stranger and a sojourner with you: give me a possession of a buryingplace with you, that I may bury my dead out of my sight.
5   And the children of Heth answered Abraham, saying unto him,
6   Hear us, my lord: you *are* a mighty prince among us: in the choice of our sepulchres bury your dead; none of us shall withhold from you his sepulchre, but that you may bury your dead.
7   And Abraham stood up, and bowed himself to the people of the land, *even* to the children of Heth.
8   And he communed with them, saying, If it be your mind that I should bury my dead out of my sight; hear me, and intreat for me to Ephron the son of Zohar,
9   That he may give me the cave of Machpelah, which he has, which *is* in the end of his field; for as much money as it is worth he shall give it me for a possession of a burying place amongst you.

10   And Ephron dwelt among the children of Heth: and Ephron the Hittite answered Abraham in the audience of the children of Heth, *even* of all that went in at the gate of his city, saying,

11   Nay, my lord, hear me: the field give I you, and the cave that *is* therein, I give it you; in the presence of the sons of my people give I it you: bury your dead.

12   And Abraham bowed down himself before the people of the land.

13   And he spoke unto Ephron in the audience of the people of the land, saying, But if you *will give it*, I pray you, hear me: I will give you money for the field; take *it* of me, and I will bury my dead there.

14   And Ephron answered Abraham, saying unto him,

15   My lord, listen unto me: the land *is worth* four hundred shekels of silver; what *is* that between me and you? bury therefore your dead.

16   And Abraham listened unto Ephron; and Abraham weighed to Ephron the silver, which he had named in the audience of the sons of Heth, four hundred shekels of silver, current *money* with the merchant.

17   And the field of Ephron, which *was* in Machpelah, which *was* before Mamre, the field, and the cave which *was* therein, and all the trees that *were* in the field, that *were* in all the borders round about, were made sure

18   Unto Abraham for a possession in the presence of the children of Heth, before all that went in at the gate of his city.

19   And after this, Abraham buried Sarah his wife in the cave of the field of Machpelah before Mamre: the same *is* Hebron in the land of Canaan.

20   And the field, and the cave that *is* therein, were made sure unto Abraham for a possession of a burying place by the sons of Heth.

Abraham lost his wife. This is a record of mourning and taking care of the business of the death of his beloved Sarah. The business of death has not changed much. You need to buy burial plots, sepulchers, or places to hold the ashes. Abraham did not take the burying for free, even though it was offered. That could incur a required return of a favor. Abraham was wise enough to know better.

One entire chapter of Genesis is dedicated to the burial of Sarah. This speaks volumes to who she was to both Abraham and God.

Dear Lord Jesus,

You are the one who conquered death! Lord, may you continue to watch over us and plan for us. For your plans are better than anything we can create. Help us to seek Your will and not own our own.

In Jesus name, Amen.

DAY #62
GENESIS 24:1-27

1   And Abraham was old, *and* well stricken in age: and the LORD had blessed Abraham in all things.
2   And Abraham said unto his eldest servant of his house, that ruled over all that he had, Put, I pray you, your hand under my thigh:

3   And I will make you swear by the LORD, the God of heaven, and the God of the earth, that you shall not take a wife unto my son of the daughters of the Canaanites, among whom I dwell:

4   But you shall go unto my country, and to my kindred, and take a wife unto my son Isaac.

5   And the servant said unto him, Peradventure the woman will not be willing to follow me unto this land: must I needs bring your son again unto the land from whence you came?

6   And Abraham said unto him, Beware you that you bring not my son there again.

7   The LORD God of heaven, which took me from my father's house, and from the land of my kindred, and which spoke unto me, and that swore unto me, saying, Unto your seed will I give this land; he shall send his angel before you, and you shall take a wife unto my son from there.

8   And if the woman will not be willing to follow you, then you shall be clear from this my oath: only bring not my son thither again.

9   And the servant put his hand under the thigh of Abraham his master, and swore to him concerning that matter.

10   And the servant took ten camels of the camels of his master, and departed; for all the goods of his master *were* in his hand: and he arose, and went to Mesopotamia, unto the city of Nahor.

11   And he made his camels to kneel down outside the city by a well of water at the time of the evening, *even* the time that women go out to draw *water*.

12   And he said, O LORD God of my master Abraham, I pray you, send me good speed this day, and show kindness unto my master Abraham.

13   Behold, I stand *here* by the well of water; and the daughters of the men of the city come out to draw water:

14   And let it come to pass, that the damsel to whom I shall say, Let down your pitcher, I pray you, that I may drink; and she shall say, Drink, and I will give your camels drink also: *let the same be* she *that* you *have* appointed for your servant Isaac; and thereby shall I know that you *have* shown kindness unto my master.

15   And it came to pass, before he had done speaking, that, behold, Rebekah came out, who was born to Bethuel, son of Milcah, the wife of Nahor, Abraham's brother, with her pitcher upon her shoulder.

16   And the damsel *was* very fair to look upon, a virgin, neither had any man known her: and she went down to the well, and filled her pitcher, and came up.

17   And the servant ran to meet her, and said, Let me, I pray you, drink a little water of your pitcher.

18   And she said, Drink, my lord: and she hasted, and let down her pitcher upon her hand, and gave him drink.

19   And when she had done giving him drink, she said, I will draw *water* for your camels also, until they have done drinking.

20   And she hasted, and emptied her pitcher into the trough, and ran again unto the well to draw *water*, and drew for all his camels.

21   And the man wondering at her held his peace, to wit whether the LORD had made his journey prosperous or not.

22   And it came to pass, as the camels had done drinking, that the man took a golden earring of half a shekel weight, and two bracelets for her hands of ten *shekels* weight of gold;

23   And said, Whose daughter *are* you? tell me, I pray you: is there room *in* your father's house for us to lodge in?

24   And she said unto him, I *am* the daughter of Bethuel the son of Milcah, which she bare unto Nahor.

25   She said moreover unto him, We have both straw and provender enough, and room to lodge in.
26   And the man bowed down his head, and worshipped the LORD.
27   And he said, Blessed *be* the LORD God of my master Abraham, who has not left destitute my master of his mercy and his truth: I *being* in the way, the LORD led me to the house of my master's brethren.

Imagine being sent to fulfill a man's last wish and you have no idea if this is even possible. But you go, because it is his wish and his love of God is infectious. This man you love for showing you God is real, in this wish trusts you with the life of his son. You go and seek the wife for his son, you get to where he said to go and pray. THEN EVERYTHING HAPPENS! God answered your prayer about things happening quickly! What can you think but God made you part of HIS plan!

What is humorous that you may not know is that Muslims claim Isaac married an infant. Really? Ever heard of an infant carrying water home, or pouring water for camels until they were done drinking? This is another example of God knowing the foolishness of false religions like Islam before it was imagined.

Dear Lord Jesus,

Sometimes we feel so blessed to see something or be part of something You are doing. We forget that You have always made us a part of Your plans. You never once left us out! This is You first loving us! Lord, please do use me to bring others to your love.

In Jesus name, Amen.

DAY #63
GENESIS 24:28-31

28   And the damsel ran, and told *them of* her mother's house these things.
29   And Rebekah had a brother, and his name *was* Laban: and Laban ran out unto the man, unto the well.
30   And it came to pass, when he saw the earring and bracelets upon his sister's hands, and when he heard the words of Rebekah his sister, saying, Thus spoke the man unto me; that he came unto the man; and, behold, he stood by the camels at the well.
31   And he said, Come in, you blessed of the LORD; Why do you stand outside? for I have prepared the house, and room for the camels.

Rebekah, ran home to get permission for this stranger to stay the night, and for his camels to be kept. She also had quite the story to share! A man gave her jewelry and praised God after she did something she quite likely normally did. She sounds young running and ambitious to make others happy. Can you imagine her excitement when she does meet those in her family and what she would say?

Sometimes I wonder why the Bible is not used in English classes when they teach about "foreshadowing." Laban, the brother of Rebekah, is here seen as the head of the family. It is likely that Abraham's nephew, Laban, and Rebkah's father, Bethuel died, and Laban is now the head of the family. Notice that Laban's eyes fall on, "the gifts" before he takes an action of kindness. It is not just his sister's words, it is the sight of the gold and jewelry that led him to call in Abraham's servant. This makes you think that Laban is greedy. Some say, "seeing is believing." Maybe that was what it was. Regardless, Laban is suddenly eager suddenly to meet this man and have him stay. These are not the type of gifts that were given casually. They are the things one gives to establish a person's wealth, status, and ability to provide – a gift to announce an intention.

Dear Lord Jesus,

The details in Your Word speak volumes. They speak of Your planning, Your working to make things happen despite the ways of the world. Lord, please use me in Your plans. Please keep working on me and making into a better example of Your love.

In Jesus name, Amen.

Dear Lord Jesus,

You include us in YOUR plans. You love us so much to allow us to see the joy and excitement in a woman who is to be the wife of Isaac. Lord, you match us with our spouses. We may claim we chose each other, but it is You alone who provide the blessings.

In Jesus name, Amen.

DAY #64
GENESIS 24:32-61

32 And the man came into the house: and he ungirded his camels, and gave straw and provender for the camels, and water to wash his feet, and the men's feet that *were* with him.
33 And there was set *meat* before him to eat: but he said, I will not eat, until I have told mine errand. And he said, Speak on.
34 And he said, I *am* Abraham's servant.
35 And the LORD has blessed my master greatly; and he is become great: and he has given him flocks, and herds, and silver, and gold, and menservants, and maidservants, and camels, and asses.
36 And Sarah my master's wife bare a son to my master when she was old: and unto him has he given all that he has.
37 And my master made me swear, saying, You shall not take a wife to my son of the daughters of the Canaanites, in whose land I dwell:
38 But you shall go unto my father's house, and to my kindred, and take a wife unto my son.
39 And I said unto my master, Peradventure the woman will not follow me.
40 And he said unto me, The LORD, before whom I walk, will send his angel with you, and prosper your way; and you shall take a wife for my son of my kindred, and of my father's house:

41   Then shall you be clear from *this* my oath, when you come to my kindred; and if they give not you *one*, you shall be clear from my oath.

42   And I came this day unto the well, and said, O LORD God of my master Abraham, if now you do prosper my way which I go:

43   Behold, I stand by the well of water; and it shall come to pass, that when the virgin comes forth to draw *water*, and I say to her, Give me, I pray you, a little water of your pitcher to drink;

44   And she say to me, Both drink you, and I will also draw for your camels: *let* the same *be* the woman whom the LORD has appointed out for my master's son.

45   And before I had done speaking in mine heart, behold, Rebekah came forth with her pitcher on her shoulder; and she went down unto the well, and drew *water*: and I said unto her, Let me drink, I pray you.

46   And she made haste, and let down her pitcher from her *shoulder*, and said, Drink, and I will give your camels drink also: so I drank, and she made the camels drink also.

47   And I asked her, and said, Whose daughter *are* you? And she said, The daughter of Bethuel, Nahor's son, whom Milcah bare unto him: and I put the earring upon her face, and the bracelets upon her hands.

48   And I bowed down my head, and worshipped the LORD, and blessed the LORD God of my master Abraham, which had led me in the right way to take my master's brother's daughter unto his son.

49   And now if you will deal kindly and truly with my master, tell me: and if not, tell me; that I may turn to the right hand, or to the left.

50 Then Laban and Bethuel answered and said, The thing proceeds from the LORD: we cannot speak unto you bad or good.

51 Behold, Rebekah *is* before you, take *her*, and go, and let her be your master's son's wife, as the LORD has spoken.

52 And it came to pass, that, when Abraham's servant heard their words, he worshipped the LORD, *bowing himself* to the earth.

53 And the servant brought forth jewels of silver, and jewels of gold, and raiment, and gave *them* to Rebekah: he gave also to her brother and to her mother precious things.

54 And they did eat and drink, he and the men that *were* with him, and tarried all night; and they rose up in the morning, and he said, Send me away unto my master.

55 And her brother and her mother said, Let the damsel abide with us *a few* days, at the least ten; after that she shall go.

56 And he said unto them, Hinder me not, seeing the LORD has prospered my way; send me away that I may go to my master.

57 And they said, We will call the damsel, and enquire at her mouth.

58 And they called Rebekah, and said unto her, Will you go with this man? And she said, I will go.

59 And they sent away Rebekah their sister, and her nurse, and Abraham's servant, and his men.

60 And they blessed Rebekah, and said unto her, You *are* our sister, be you *the mother* of thousands of millions, and let your seed possess the gate of those which hate them.

61 And Rebekah arose, and her damsels, and they rode upon the camels, and followed the man: and the servant took Rebekah, and went his way.

Finally, Bethuel is brought to the scene. As the father of Rebekah, he should be the one to give her away. Laban has appeared as the head of the family, and Bethuel and Laban approve of a family decision. This speaks to Laban being the current head of the family, and his father being elderly in need of assistance, just like Abraham. Note that Bethuel is considerably younger than Abraham at that time. They do not deny that the story is proof of God's hand in locating Rebekah.

The servant here is proven to have well-earned Abraham's trust. He does not delay in his task. He is asked to stay a few days. This again is the foreshadowing of sadness to come. His refusal to delay his task places one more need for things to be final. Rebekah's own approval. Which she gives.

Now things get interesting. Not only does she come, but "her damsels." Can you imagine the flurry of activity with women deciding what to bring with them NOW for a journey they will not return from? In this passage, one of them was her nurse. This was likely a person who served as a nanny. She was not without wealth also, so with her came servants. This was likely a surprise to be escorting more than Rebekah back, but remember Abraham's servant did not come alone, he brought other women to ensure a safe return for the bride of Isaac. They just did not expect to bring other women with them.

Do not forget that this was a LONG journey. Abraham's servant never let the frailness of his loved master, leave him. It kept the sense of urgency alive in him. His men also must have felt a sense of unrest and eagerness to return. This may have been a seemingly short meeting. A rushed gathering of things by Rebekah and the women who came with her also. It was but a brief stop accomplishing a task that God made them part of.

Dear Lord Jesus,

You are the one who shows us Your love, by being active in our lives each day! It never ceases to amaze me how many seemingly impossible things happen because of Your love. Lord Jesus, just as this servant was obedient and was urgent in doing the will of his master, Lord give me that sense of urgency to share Your love. Direct me so that I may be used also.

In Jesus name, Amen.

DAY #65
GENESIS 24:62-67

62   And Isaac came from the way of the well Lahairoi; for he dwelt in the south country.
63   And Isaac went out to meditate in the field at the eventide: and he lifted up his eyes, and saw, and, behold, the camels *were* coming.
64   And Rebekah lifted up her eyes, and when she saw Isaac, she lighted off the camel.
65   For she *had* said unto the servant, What man *is* this that walks in the field to meet us? And the servant *had* said, It *is* my master: therefore she took a vail, and covered herself.
66   And the servant told Isaac all things that he had done.
67   And Isaac brought her into his mother Sarah's tent, and took Rebekah, and she became his wife; and he loved her: and Isaac was comforted after his mother's *death*.

BAM! This is a story that sounds like love at first sight! Rebekkah sees him and is immediately interested. Isaac sees her approaching on a camel and has to know why the camels are approaching and sees Rebekah. He wants to see her better the two practically fell in love at first sight. Isaac took her into his mother's tent. He lifted her up above all the other women there! He gave her all he could that he could think that she might like. Now think about this. His mother has been dead for a while. He knew the purpose of his father's servant going back to the homeland. This would mean that Isaac prepared for his bride's return. This explains the purpose of going to his mother's tent instead of his own. He was faithful, believing God would make this trip profitable! That means he fully believed the woman who would be brought back would be his future bride. Isaac loved her!

Dear Lord Jesus,

Chance meetings, when arranged by you are divine appointments with divine rewards! Sometimes we just need to think back to things in our lives that seemed simple, to realize how much you made happen for that one thing to happen. Lord, you deserve our praises and worship for loving us so much that you get involved in our lives. You do so much for us without claiming glory. Lord, You have my love and I ask that You make me more like You.

In Jesus name, Amen.

DAY #66
GENESIS 25:1-10

1 Then again Abraham took a wife, and her name *was* Keturah.
2 And she bare him Zimran, and Jokshan, and Medan, and Midian, and Ishbak, and Shuah.
3 And Jokshan begat Sheba, and Dedan. And the sons of Dedan were Asshurim, and Letushim, and Leummim.
4 And the sons of Midian; Ephah, and Epher, and Hanoch, and Abida, and Eldaah. All these *were* the children of Keturah.
5 And Abraham gave all that he had unto Isaac.
6 But unto the sons of the concubines, which Abraham had, Abraham gave gifts, and sent them away from Isaac his son, while he yet lived, eastward, unto the east country.
7 And these *are* the days of the years of Abraham's life which he lived, an hundred threescore and fifteen years.
8 Then Abraham gave up the ghost, and died in a good old age, an old man, and full *of years*; and was gathered to his people.
9 And his sons Isaac and Ishmael buried him in the cave of Machpelah, in the field of Ephron the son of Zohar the Hittite, which *is* before Mamre;
10 The field which Abraham purchased of the sons of Heth: there was Abraham buried, and Sarah his wife.

Here we learn that Abraham while he had seemed on his deathbed when he sent his servant to find Isaac a wife, revived with vigor when Rebekah was brought back to Isaac. Abraham took time to learn things, like most of us. Maybe he needed to feel near death, to seek out a wife for his son, considering Isaac was forty. Then doing that, God returned his strength to him.

Matthew Henry speaks of Abraham in his later days as a man of seclusion since we know very little of those days outside of his marriage to Keturah, who was likely one of the maidservants. Keturah actually gives birth to one who is to be the father of the people known today as Arabs. We can see that in verse 6.

When it is Abraham's time to pass away he is 175 years old. This means Abraham lived another thirty-five years after Isaac took Rebekah as his wife. Matthew Henry points out four things about Abraham's death:

1. *He gave up the ghost*. His life was not extorted from him, but he cheerfully resigned it; into the hands of the Father of spirits, he committed his spirit.
2. *He died in a good old age, an old man*; so God had promised him. His death was his discharge from the burdens of his age: an old man would not so live always. It was also the crown of the glory of his old age.
3. *He was full of years,* or *full of life* (as it might be supplied), including all the conveniences and comforts of life. He did not live till the world was weary of him, but till he was weary of the world; he had had enough of it and desired no more. Vixi quantum satis est – I have lived long enough. A good man, though he should not die old, dies full of days, satisfied with living here, and longing to live in a better place.
4. *He was gathered to his people.* His body was gathered to the congregation of the dead, and his soul to the congregation of the blessed. Note, Death gathers us into our people. Those who are our people while we live, whether the people of God or the children of this world are the people to whom death will gather us.

Dear Lord Jesus,

You provide so much to us that we cannot comprehend how much you give us. Lord God, You show us examples of how to live with a great man like Abraham. Examples that are not perfect, but men who are fallible, who made stupid mistakes just like us. This makes me, even more, ask of you to not stop working on me. You are the potter, keep molding me and making me better!

In Jesus name, Amen.

DAY #67
GENESIS 25:11-18

11 And it came to pass after the death of Abraham, that God blessed his son Isaac; and Isaac dwelt by the well Lahairoi.
12 Now these *are* the generations of Ishmael, Abraham's son, whom Hagar the Egyptian, Sarah's handmaid, bare unto Abraham:
13 And these *are* the names of the sons of Ishmael, by their names, according to their generations: the firstborn of Ishmael, Nebajoth; and Kedar, and Adbeel, and Mibsam,
14 And Mishma, and Dumah, and Massa,
15 Hadar, and Tema, Jetur, Naphish, and Kedemah:
16 These *are* the sons of Ishmael, and these *are* their names, by their towns, and by their castles; twelve princes according to their nations.

17   And these *are* the years of the life of Ishmael, an hundred and thirty and seven years: and he gave up the ghost and died; and was gathered unto his people.
18   And they dwelt from Havilah unto Shur, that *is* before Egypt, as you goes toward Assyria: *and* he died in the presence of all his brethren.

Did you know about the twelve tribes (nations) of Ishmael? Remember, God rejected Ishmael as a human attempt to fulfill God's blessing rather than waiting for God's blessing.

Ishmael had received a blessing given to his mother in Genesis 16:10,

> "And the angel of the LORD said unto her, I will multiply your seed exceedingly, that it shall not be numbered for multitude."

Abraham also sought God and asked him to bless Ishmael, in Genesis 17:20,

> "And as for Ishmael, I have heard you: Behold, I have blessed him, and will make him fruitful, and will multiply him exceedingly; twelve princes shall he beget, and I will make him a great nation."

God fulfilled this promise quickly, creating a nation out of Ishmael. It would not be until the next generation that God would create Israel. This was a blessing sought where man inserted his will to create a blessing when God was in the business of perfect timing. Ishmael had a blessing, but in comparison to the one given to Isaac, it still is miniscule. Who can claim to be a child of Ishmael today vs. who can claim to be a child of Isaac? Muslims from Saudi Arabia claim to be descended from Ishmael. But Keturah's children were there. Not Hagar's son. The lineage there is a fable. It is not established.

This should be a lesson about legacy. Do not try to replace what God has promised with a vain attempt at fulfillment.

Dear Lord Jesus,

Who are we in comparison to You? We are imperfect. We are sinful. We may seek You but we often also do what is wrong. Lord, we need Your divine touch on us, that we may be continually changed and molded after Your image. Lord, please do not stop working on me!

In Jesus name, Amen.

DAY #68
GENESIS 25:19-26

19 And these *are* the generations of Isaac, Abraham's son: Abraham begat Isaac:
20 And Isaac was forty years old when he took Rebekah to wife, the daughter of Bethuel the Syrian of Padanaram, the sister to Laban the Syrian.
21 And Isaac intreated the LORD for his wife, because she *was* barren: and the LORD was intreated of him, and Rebekah his wife conceived.

22   And the children struggled together within her; and she said, If *it be* so, why *am* I thus? And she went to enquire of the LORD.

23   And the LORD said unto her, Two nations *are* in your womb, and two manner of people shall be separated from your bowels; and *the one* people shall be stronger than *the other* people; and the elder shall serve the younger.

24   And when her days to be delivered were fulfilled, behold, *there were* twins in her womb.

25   And the first came out red, all over like an hairy garment; and they called his name Esau.

26   And after that came his brother out, and his hand took hold on Esau's heel; and his name was called Jacob: and Isaac *was* threescore years old when she bare them.

For nineteen years Rebekah did not have a child. Women who are barren understand that difficulty as something oppressive and very real. Isaac knew he was to have a child. It was already promised to his father! He would have been told about how long his mother and father waited for his birth. This makes you wonder if Isaac waited a long time to start to seek God on this. Notice verse 21 states "Isaac intreated the LORD for his wife, because she *was* barren: and the LORD was intreated of him, and Rebekah his wife conceived." This seems immediate. It is also a sign of Isaac's faith in that promise.

Now, can you imagine the tussle of two within a womb, kicking and punching for space to grow and live? Worse, can you imagine being the woman who has to endure that burden within you? Today, doctors prescribe bedrest to women with difficult pregnancies. She likely has observed many women in the past twenty years during pregnancy and in giving birth. She probably asked them many questions, and nothing they could tell her addressed the difficulties she felt. So, Rebekah goes to God in prayer about this. She is worried something is very wrong.

God's answer, has to surprise her. Twin births were and still are somewhat uncommon. More importantly, what did Rebekah do with what she heard from God? We are not given that answer. Did she tell her husband or someone else at that time? We can never know the answer. What is clear, is that there still is an order of birth with twins. The older one, never lets the younger one forget who was first. Rebekah was told the older one would serve the younger one. She tucked this into her heart and did everything she could to assist and improve the younger one until her dying day.

Dear Lord Jesus,

It's humorous how we so often tell You how should it go, and you have to set us straight. You told Rebekah how things would be. Yet Isaac set his heart on his eldest inheriting a blessing and the leadership role of the family, as was the custom of the day. Lord, make me listen like Rebekah and work to see Your plan unfold.

In Jesus name, Amen.

DAY #69
GENESIS 25:27-34

27 And the boys grew: and Esau was a cunning hunter, a man of the field; and Jacob *was* a plain man, dwelling in tents.

28 And Isaac loved Esau, because he did eat of *his* venison: but Rebekah loved Jacob.
29 And Jacob sod pottage: and Esau came from the field, and he *was* faint:
30 And Esau said to Jacob, Feed me, I pray you, with that same red *pottage*; for I *am* faint: therefore was his name called Edom.
31 And Jacob said, Sell me this day your birthright.
32 And Esau said, Behold, I *am* at the point to die: and what profit shall this birthright do to me?
33 And Jacob said, Swear to me this day; and he swore unto him: and he sold his birthright unto Jacob.
34 Then Jacob gave Esau bread and pottage of lentiles; and he did eat and drink, and rose up, and went his way: thus Esau despised *his* birthright.

This story tells us who the two boys became as young men. They were opposites. One was favored over the other by each parent. Isaac was the one God chose and mostly lived as an only child. Rebekah seems younger than her brother Laban and also could have experienced that, but had seen her brother as the favored one to receive the birthright as head of the family. Today, parents strive, to not play favorites.

The sibling rivalry saw Esau winning most if not all the physical contests between them. They were boys, they would have raced, they would have competed daily. Even to the stage of this story. The one thing Jacob knew that separated them was Esau being born first. Tradition made sure that the firstborn got it all. Jacob would be second, which meant last when there were only two competing.

Jacob was one who watched, he listened, he observed. He learned to cook, something considered a woman's duty during that time. He coveted that birthright Esau had. He thought about it as the one thing that would let him win in the end. He knew his brother loved being free with nothing to tie him down. He also knew his brother never really learned how to cook so he came home from every hunt mad with hunger.

Can you imagine Esau returning from a hunt, his stomach craving food, and smelling something so wonderful he just had to taste it—no, he wanted to satisfy his hunger from that wonderful scent in the air of great food. Esau was first born, he could say, "do this and go there," and people would obey. He was a prince in many ways, except he could not order his twin brother to do things. He probably raced in towards the smell of the soup, ready to demand one of the women who cooked the food, to give it to him. But found his brother as the cook – the one person he could not demand things from.

Jacob, asked a steep price for the bowl of soup and bread, "give me your birthright." Without a thought, it was given. NO banter over the price – it was given!

Position in a family is not something thought of today as something that can be bought or sold. You can't change your birth order. But, during the time of Esau and Jacob, birthrights could be sold. This right was to be the head of the family. The one to make the decisions. The one to inherit the most. What does this say about what Esau thought of his family, much less God?

Dear Lord Jesus,

Help me to think about the things that are of importance to You before I think about things that seem important to me. Lord, you are the one who knows best. You are the one who gives the best gifts. Lord, I want to seek after Your will, not my own. I don't want to pursue my own selfish desires. I would that my desires would not be vain things, but that they would be pleasing to You. Lord, please keep working on me.

In Jesus name, Amen.

Bibliography

Hassett, B., & Sağlamtimur, H. (2018, June 27). Radical 'royals'? Burial practices at Başur Höyük and the emergence of early states in Mesopotamia. *Antiquity*, 640 – 654. Retrieved from https://www.cambridge.org/core/journals/antiquity/article/abs/radical-royals-burial-practices-at-basur-hoyuk-and-the-emergence-of-early-states-in-mesopotamia/23E69D907B072E3789DC5B4F72108AC6

www.ingramcontent.com/pod-product-compliance
Lightning Source LLC
LaVergne TN
LVHW010218070526
838199LV00062B/4646